big
plans
small
gardens

big
plans
small
gardens

andy sturgeon
gold medal-winning garden designer

MITCHELL BEAZLEY

Big Plans Small Gardens

by Andy Sturgeon

First published in Great Britain in 2010 by Mitchell Beazley,
an imprint of Octopus Publishing Group Limited,
2–4 Heron Quays, London E14 4JP.
www.octopusbooks.co.uk

An Hachette Livre Company
www.hachettelivre.co.uk

Distributed in the United States and Canada by Octopus Books USA
c/o Hachette Book Group USA, 237 Park Avenue, New York, NY 10017
www.octopusbooksusa.com

The publishers will be grateful for any information that will assist them in
keeping future editions up to date. Although all reasonable care has been
taken in the preparation of this book, neither the publishers nor the author
can accept any liability for any consequence arising from the use thereof,
or the information contained therein.

The author has asserted his moral rights.

ISBN: 978 1 84533 372 0

A CIP record for this book is available from the British Library.

Set in Helvetica Neue.

Colour reproduction by Fine Arts in Hong Kong.
Printed and bound by Toppan Printing Company in China.

Commissioning Editor Helen Griffin
Senior Editor Leanne Bryan
Copy Editor Helen Ridge
Proofreader Ruth Baldwin
Indexer Diana Lecore
Art Directors Tim Foster and Pene Parker
Senior Art Editor Victoria Easton
Designer Sarah Rock
Picture Research Manager Giulia Hetherington
Production Manager Peter Hunt

Contents

Introduction

They've come a long way, gardens. I can remember when they were just about growing stuff; all lawns and plants and precious little else. But now the very notion of what makes a garden has been turned on its head. The idea that they should be some sort of horticultural zoo is virtually redundant as our gardens have become far more to do with lifestyle. We want an outdoor kitchen, a living room, dining room and playroom; somewhere to entertain, somewhere to escape to and maybe even somewhere to impress our friends (go on, admit it). We may even want to grow a few plants as well. But for many of us outdoor space is limited and the demands we place upon it are huge, so in order for a small garden to be successful, it has to be very carefully thought out.

Although we may crave a garden the size of a football pitch, I genuinely believe that some of the smallest gardens are among the best. The lack of space seems to force creativity and ingenuity; it demands lateral thinking and experimentation, often with extraordinary results. By their very nature, small gardens are likely to have problems – apart from a lack of room, they may also suffer from a lack of light or soil, they may be sandwiched between buildings or be virtually inaccessible. What unites all the gardens in this book is that these often uninspiring places have been transformed and their shortcomings turned into incredible attributes.

Deciding how you want your garden to look is the first step, and probably the hardest. Once you have established this, I urge you to stick to it. Keep to the vision and don't stray off the path. Next, you have to decide what to put into the garden, while acknowledging that there is a significant difference between what you want and what you need.

The temptation is to cram everything you can into what little space you have, but one of the first rules of design is that you should pare down your ideas. It's a bit like packing to go on holiday – you want to take everything, just in case, but once you get to the hotel, you realize that a pair of

shorts, a few t-shirts and your sunglasses are all you really need. Good design is actually about the editing of ideas, and what you leave out is just as important as what you include. So examine the way you live, decide how you will use the garden and even how you will look after it.

There's a minefield of information out there, and the more you look, the more ideas you'll have. I hope that this book will offer up some solutions and help to galvanize your thoughts so that you develop a clear direction that suits your outside space, no matter where it is, how small it is and however you intend to use it.

The case studies featured throughout the book cover virtually every scenario you are likely to encounter and they can be mimicked down to the tiniest detail or reinterpreted to suit your particular space. Alternatively, ideas can be cherry-picked, but remember that design doesn't work if it is simply just copied without any understanding.

There was a celebrated 20th-century Mexican architect and landscape designer called Luis Barragán, who was a master of space, light and colour. His work is known by just about every student of those disciplines and it is frequently copied but often without a great deal of success. He was famously quoted as saying, "Don't do what I do, see what I see." I have always remembered that instruction and, even when flicking through the pages here, I feel it's important to have at least some basic level of comprehension of the ideas on offer before they can be translated into a new garden. With that in mind, I have endeavoured to explain the thought processes behind the pictures.

In the end, though, planning a garden should be simple and enjoyable. What we have here are realistic solutions that exemplify outstanding design. These will help you to set your sights high and create the very best garden that you can.

ANDY STURGEON

WHAT IS IT YOU WANT?

We all use our gardens differently, so, before you make any rash design decisions, take a good look at how you live. Will the garden be used primarily for entertaining or for sunbathing, drinking a glass of wine or, heaven forbid, even doing some gardening? You really have only one shot at this, so you need to get it right from the outset.

ABOVE Modern grass planting completes the contemporary look of this roof terrace, especially when complemented by a cast-aluminium table and chairs.

BELOW Large, well-designed pieces of modular furniture are part of a garden's structure and can be arranged just as they would be in a room. The tree provides useful shade.

RIGHT If space is limited, chairs need to be upright enough to be suitable for dining and sufficiently comfortable for sitting on for a considerable length of time. Showerproof soft furnishings are essential.

ABOVE Tables and chairs should always have plenty of space around them so that people can come and go without squeezing past others.

Eating and entertaining

Unless you are a hard-core gardener, you are likely to spend a large amount of your time in the garden sitting down, relaxing and entertaining. By its very nature, a dining area has to be near to the kitchen and, for easy access, close to the doors into the garden. This means that the outdoor space has to be very functional and must also look the part, with the furniture itself being integral to the whole feel and style of the garden. Versatility is paramount. A seating area that can routinely accommodate the whole family and maybe a few friends must also be flexible enough to be adapted for entertaining and parties, yet still be intimate enough for a person to sit quietly on their own.

RIGHT The large, L-shaped bench seat can accommodate lots of extra people while entertaining but the two individual chairs are more comfortable for everyday dining.

GETTING SEATED

In a small garden, the seating area may dominate or, at least, influence the entire design. So think of it as part of the garden's architecture and let its shape and materials dictate what you design elsewhere. The worst mistake you can make is to design the space first, then look for furniture afterwards. A holistic approach is essential.

FIRST THINGS FIRST

The materials you choose are a major part of the design process. When deciding on a colour palette for the hard landscaping, you should take the furniture into consideration. A wooden table, for example, may harmonize well with the natural colours and materials you intend to use for the paving and wall surfaces. On the other hand, if you want to give the garden a more contemporary edge, consider glass and metal.

An element of bespoke, built-in seating helps to marry the area to the overall design. A simple bench, for instance, is easily connected to a retaining wall or planter and suddenly everything becomes integrated.

Plants are useful too; after all, this is a garden and not just another room. But a word of caution: choose your plants carefully or you will forever be pruning them out of the way or clearing up dead leaves and other debris.

However, the most important thing to consider is space, and it is vital that you build in enough at the planning stage. There is nothing worse than clambering over each other to get out from the dining table or having people squeeze past behind chairs.

ABOVE An outdoor bar with built-in fridges and storage underneath may be a good idea for frequent entertaining but the design still needs to work well even when there isn't a party.

LEFT If comfort is a priority, choose showerproof cushions. These can be left outside for much of the time and stored indoors only during the worst weather. The frames of these seats are synthetic, so they can remain *in situ*.

OPPOSITE As a rule, people prefer to eat in the shade, perhaps under a canopy, which can also keep out rain and create some essential privacy.

CONSIDER THIS

- Built-in seating combined with free-standing, stackable chairs offers maximum versatility, giving you the best of both worlds for dining and relaxation.

- Low walls and steps can double up as occasional seating so you don't have to worry about storing extra chairs.

- People generally prefer to dine in the shade but, even in a tiny garden, it is nice to have the option of sun. If you use canopies, check that you can take them down.

- For convenience, position dining tables as near as possible to the kitchen.

- Lighting is absolutely essential for entertaining at night. Mount it high if you want to be able to see your food. If you wish, supplement electric lighting with candles and lanterns.

- Make sure that the space is uncluttered. People need to be able to move around easily without squeezing past furniture, falling in ponds or dropping off the edge of a terrace.

- If space is severely limited, forget about having a separate outside dining table, especially if the garden leads directly off a dining room or kitchen.

- Storage for cushions and other paraphernalia can influence furniture choices. A storage chest can double up as a bench.

- Consider materials carefully and harmonize them with features and surfaces in the garden. Be aware, though, that different materials will age and weather at varying rates over time.

FLEXIBLE FURNITURE

The furniture you choose must be appropriate to how you intend to use your outdoor entertaining space. For example, if you live alone but on occasions like to hold big parties, you have different needs at opposite ends of the spectrum, which may necessitate some form of compromise. It would be foolish to introduce a huge number of chairs that would seldom be sat on. The solution is to go for flexibility. Cater for your day-to-day needs first – perhaps a table and a few chairs – but build in occasional seating. This could be low retaining walls or planters set at a comfortable seat height – 45–50cm (18–20in) high – which would allow a number of people to perch on them if the conventional seats were to run out. Walls should be wide enough – ideally 30cm (12in) – to accommodate the average buttocks.

Steps can also be used for seating, but make sure they are wide enough to allow people to pass, as constantly having to move out of the way of others is irritating. Don't overlook comfort. Do you want to dine in an upright chair or relax in something softer? Stools and benches are economical with space but most adults won't want to sit on them for too long.

SURFACE AREAS

Surfaces are important for resting drinks and plates on. Again, this could be the top of walls but perhaps higher – table height is around 70cm (28in) and worktop height closer to 90cm (35in). The surface should be flat to avoid balancing wine glasses precariously. If you don't want glasses teetering on a balcony rail, where they could be easily knocked off, make it rounded or too narrow for them to fit.

ABOVE A small low table and matching stools take up very little space and are perfect for enjoying a coffee or a glass of wine. They would not, though, be sufficiently comfortable for relaxed dining.

CHECKLIST

HOW DO YOU ENTERTAIN?

- Do you live alone? ☐
- Do you entertain regularly? ☐
- Do you have a large family? ☐
- What is your priority: dining or informal entertaining? ☐
- Will you eat and entertain mostly in the evenings, daytime or both? ☐
- What is more useful: formal dining chairs or more comfortable seating? ☐

RIGHT A warm sunny wall will absorb heat during the day. As the wall cools down in the evening, it can actually raise the temperature around it by a few degrees.

BELOW RIGHT Suspended by chains, this simple table is raised up so people can sit on the surrounding deck and swing their legs into the space underneath.

Words of wisdom

- The ideal place for an eating area is a warm sunny spot that offers a degree of privacy as well as shelter from the wind. Existing trees or shrubs may provide this or you may need to incorporate a canopy.

- A water feature close to the seating area can double up as a convenient wine chiller.

- Deep down, all humans are lazy creatures, so any dining table has to be as near to the kitchen as possible. Fortunately, this also makes practical sense.

CASE STUDY: **Rooftop entertaining**

ASPECT This city apartment measures barely 5 x 5m (16 x 16ft), faces north and is reasonably sunny during the summer. There are good views to the west, with no tall buildings close enough to invade the privacy, while to the north there are some unsightly offices and a future development planned. Overall the garden is quite sheltered.

BRIEF A terrace leading directly off the living room, to be used as a contemporary outside dining area for the summer months, was requested. The priorities were to accommodate up to eight people comfortably, while also providing a sensible, practical space for the couple who live here. The garden needed to incorporate a sizeable amount of planting and to disguise the very rectangular shape of the roof. Running water was to be included to muffle the sound of the traffic below. Screening from neighbouring buildings was paramount. A small rear terrace, 5m (16ft) by just over 2m (6½ft), off the bedroom was to be designed to offer a view out through the windows rather than serve any practical purpose.

Olive trees are ideal on a roof because they don't mind the drying effects of wind and sun, and can live quite happily in containers, which restrict their roots.

Low planting to the rear of the seat keeps the views open and doesn't encroach upon the curved seating area.

The table is made from a single piece of limestone, which has been sealed to prevent staining from food and wine.

Because of weight restrictions and available depth, timber decking is often the only option for a roof terrace, unless the building was constructed originally to cope with thicker and heavier surfaces.

Intimate dining with style

The electrically ignited gas flambeau fires up at the flick of a switch. As well as providing warmth, it is also an innovative light source.

Decorative stainless-steel mesh like woven bamboo is mounted in powder-coated frames, to match the window frames of the building. It filters the wind and blocks ugly views.

The stainless-steel water sculpture reflects light and brightens up a wall that receives very little direct sunlight, thereby increasing the feeling of space.

These two sculptural benches enforce and echo the symmetry of the original building. They are primarily for ornamentation but can also be used as seating.

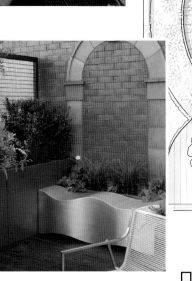

CONSIDERATIONS Since the apartment was in a converted former warehouse, the existing fabric was legally protected and had to be preserved. Nothing could be fixed to the façade or alter its appearance from street level.

DESIGN SOLUTION To reduce the impact of the severe rectangles imposed by the shape of the terrace and the building, a dramatic sweeping curve was introduced in the form of a bench seat with storage beneath. To the rear of the bench, the curve creates a deep planter, which gives you the sense of sitting right among the lush planting.

With fixed seating, it is vital that the table and bench are set far enough apart to allow people to slide in and out comfortably yet sufficiently close for eating a meal

without having to lean too far forward. Curved seating is infinitely more inviting than tables and chairs arranged on a rectangular grid because everyone can face each other. In this instance, the planting behind makes the space feel protected and intimate.

The gas flambeau takes the edge off the cold on chilly evenings, prolonging the use of the space. The atmospheric light that it provides is sufficient to eat by.

The mesh screens, combined with light and airy planting, retain the feeling of space, while simultaneously blocking out the adjacent buildings. This translucent wall acts like a net curtain by providing privacy.

DESIGNER Andy Sturgeon

RIGHT Natural materials are the way forward; rope and timber have been used to make a spider's-web climbing frame, which becomes an attractive feature in its own right.

CENTRE RIGHT Tree houses are limited only by your imagination, planning permission and, perhaps, your carpentry skills. If you don't have a big enough tree, build the house on stilts.

BELOW RIGHT This redundant space beneath a deck has been transformed into a den, with children's seating and a climbing wall, and also offers some privacy.

Playing

Small gardens have to be multifunctional and, as well as looking good, they may also have to be part-time playgrounds. Throw into the mix the need to keep both children and adults entertained, and you really have a design challenge on your hands. Where space is tight, you need to be at your most creative. There is nothing worse than a garden filled with brightly coloured plastic toys – you may as well grass the whole thing over and forget all about aesthetics. Keep reminding yourself that you are making a garden, not a playground.

ABOVE Play isn't just for children. Outdoor living rooms, complete with waterproof TVs and speakers, are all the rage with adults.

LEFT Children can outgrow play equipment fast, but as trampolines are enjoyed by a far wider age group than most toys, they will stay in use for a lot longer.

GETTING READY FOR PLAY

It is worth remembering that children have very fertile imaginations so don't necessarily need lots of toys. Rather they need plenty of simple things to play with and places they can call their own. The ideal play area is one where they can indulge their imaginations safely and unsupervised, so make sure that fences are secure and gates are bolted out of reach, so that little people can't wander off.

Then make the garden childproof, which means using sturdy shrubs and plants that won't get easily broken by balls and sticks and everything else. Thorns and poisonous plants should obviously be avoided.

As they grow, kids like to have their own domain, somewhere they can keep out of sight of adults. Large bushes like rhododendrons and bamboo are particularly good for making camps, allowing young eyes to peer out while inquisitive adult eyes can't penetrate the foliage from the outside. It's a sort of organic two-way mirror.

The garden structure should also be safe. It could include things to climb on like walls and raised platforms that primarily have an aesthetic or practical function but are also perfect for kids.

WHAT'S UNDER FOOT?

Surfaces can be problematic. Even small lawns can form the basis of a thousand children's games, but they can wear out fast. Use a hard-wearing grass or consider artificial grass that doesn't need mowing and won't turn into a mud patch so can be used year-round in all weathers.

Of course, adults sometimes want to play, too, and that doesn't just mean eating and entertaining (see pages 12–19). There are a few other possibilities – a pétanque court is one, made of self-binding gravel with some loose stones on the top. Pétanque can be played by both adults and children but, importantly, the surface looks good and it could double up as a path or even a seating area.

OPPOSITE ABOVE Children don't necessarily need meticulously designed playgrounds – simple elements like a swing, a ladder and some sand can keep them occupied for hours.

OPPOSITE BELOW Messy play, including painting and sandpits, is often best kept out of the house. Covered in blackboard paint, a shed wall or the inside of a sandpit lid makes an ideal blackboard.

BELOW A gravel path or a sunken terrace can double up as a pétanque court, becoming a visual asset in the garden.

KEEPING KIDS BUSY

- Solid paths are essential for children who love to trundle around on anything with wheels. If possible, make a decent circuit, otherwise they'll be forced backwards and forwards along the same path like caged animals. Incorporate slopes to avoid steps.

- Gardens should be planned around the whole family, not just the kids. If space allows, provide separate areas for adults and children but also a place where they can come together – perhaps a seating area or a lawn.

- Harness children's energy by encouraging them to garden. A place for kids to grow a few vegetables, sow some seeds and hold a sunflower-growing competition not only keeps them occupied but is also educational.

- Children discover new things every day, which helps them to develop their senses and physical skills. A garden should offer scent, colour, sound, tactile and edible delights, wildlife and a whole host of nature's pleasures.

- Attracting wildlife engages children and teaches them to respect and admire nature. They will also learn that even those things that bite and sting have their place.

- Ponds, despite the obvious potential hazards, are filled with excitement for children of all ages. It's amazing how much fun frogs, mud, dragonflies and pebbles can be.

- Hot tubs take up relatively little space but are one of the few 'toys' that can be genuinely enjoyed by both children and adults.

- A lawn is perhaps the most essential and easiest element to provide for children and adults. It can be used to pitch a tent, play ball games, picnic and sunbathe. The list is endless.

- Children yearn to investigate and this should be indulged. Try to add a sense of adventure and mystery into the design, which will encourage them to develop imaginative play.

LEFT Avoiding plastic and using timber instead means that play equipment can blend well into the garden and become part of its structure.

OUT OF SIGHT, OUT OF MIND

The garden can be divided up so that adults can sit away from children. The seating area, for example, could be a step up or down from the path that's used for cycling and skateboarding, thereby avoiding unpleasant crashes with furniture and ankles.

Play equipment can be partially screened so you can keep an eye on things without the climbing frame, say, becoming the focus of the garden. Some form of slatted screen is ideal, as it is just enough to soften outlines and colours without blocking the view.

If the play equipment is on full show, you need to think carefully about what it is made from. Bright colours are hard to blend in, which makes timber the favourite option. With careful design, it is possible to construct a play area that looks like a garden first and foremost and is actually quite attractive.

Safety steps

- A garden should keep children constructively occupied and allow them to play safely on their own without adult supervision, making everyone happy.

- In your efforts to create a completely safe garden, there is a danger of making it boring. It is now generally accepted that some element of risk is essential to a child's development.

- Avoid sharp thorns and plants that sting or have irritant sap. Highly poisonous plants should be avoided, although the reality is that children don't usually eat garden plants, so try not to be over-paranoid.

- Potentially dangerous drops can be made safer by adding railings; alternatively, plant shrubs at the top to keep children away and at the bottom to break their fall.

CHECKLIST

WHAT DO YOU WANT FOR YOUR KIDS?

- Versatile lawn ☐
- Water feature or pond ☐
- Kids' domain and adult space ☐
- A place to sow seeds ☐
- Play equipment or den ☐
- Adventure and mystery ☐
- Safety and security ☐
- Plants and wildlife ☐

Sandpits can be hidden under lids in decking or paving. Lids keep them tidy and also exclude cats. Ideally, sandpits should be raised a little so that rainwater drains out. It's also handy to have an edge or a low wall for adults to perch on. The inside of a sandpit lid can double up as a blackboard.

WAYS WITH WATER

Water in a garden can keep children entertained for hours. A pond with fish and wildlife is educational and fun, although there are safety aspects to consider. Metal mesh set just below the water surface can stop children falling in but, to be on the safe side, the actual pond or water reservoir can be hidden or filled with stone cobbles. This isn't much use for wildlife but you can still have a bubble fountain to play with. Swimming-pool chemicals can be added to the water to keep it hygienic.

STRUCTURAL THINKING

The structure of the garden can be just as important as toys or play equipment when encouraging imaginative play. If possible, keep child and adult spaces separate with some kind of physical barrier, such as a step or other subtle division.

" Planting needs to be childproof and able to withstand ball games and spontaneous deadheading "

ABOVE Swimming pools don't have to be Olympic sized to be enjoyed. If designed properly, they should be attractive features in their own right.

LEFT Tiles made from recycled rubber are easy to install and provide a safe, cushioned surface to play on.

CASE STUDY: **Good-looking and child-friendly**

ASPECT Facing east, this rectangular garden is bathed in sunshine for much of the day, until the sun dips down behind the house in mid-afternoon and casts shade over the dining area. Measuring 16 x 5m (52 x 16ft), the garden is surrounded on all sides by similar terraced houses and gardens.

BRIEF The clients wanted to create a garden that could accommodate their needs and also those of their two young children, all without sacrificing good design. Play equipment and toys needed to be hidden from view, although the children still had to be partially visible to make sure they were playing well together and not getting into any mischief. A new glazed extension on the rear of the house offered year-round views of the garden, which meant that all of it had to look good at all times. The garden was to flow out from the house and appear as a continuation of the interior design. There was to be an element of planting, although this needed to be easy to maintain and robust enough to withstand a few hard knocks from the kids.

The slatted timber screen masks off the unattractive play equipment but still allows parents to keep an eye on things.

Artificial grass has none of the maintenance headaches of real grass or the mud that inevitably gets brought into the house.

The dry rill planted with ornamental grasses cleverly demarcates the adult "kid-free" zone but can also be used for imaginative play.

The black timber deck and raised planter link the garden to the window frames and other elements of the house, effectively unifying the entire design.

Pleasing adults as well as children

Children respond well to bright colours, which can be used in a funky way without making the garden look like a nursery school.

The dead space beneath the existing tree has been turned into a versatile timber tree seat, enjoyed by both adults and children.

The gentle fountain, which bubbles up through this drilled rock, is a lot of fun for children to play with and perfectly safe.

Play equipment is rarely good-looking and should be hidden from view wherever possible.

CONSIDERATIONS To blur the division between inside and out, the deck area was stained black to echo the solid window frames of the house. The integrated storage wall running down one side of the deck works like a piece of architecture, exaggerating the effect of an outdoor room, and on the opposite boundary the wall of this open "room" is painted a warm orange. A dry "rill" of gravel and plants makes a subtle barrier sufficient to keep marauding kids at bay.

DESIGN SOLUTION The garden is loosely zoned to create a kids' play area at the rear, a predominantly adult seating and dining area near the house and a flexible area in between to suit both adults and children. The play equipment is hidden by a slatted timber screen but it still allows parents to see what's going on behind if necessary. Artificial grass was chosen because small lawns in shady gardens soon turn to mud when there are children about. This extremely low-maintenance and clean solution also removes the need for the storage of a bulky lawn mower. Since the dining table is in shade from mid-afternoon, a second seating area with a raised timber tree seat has been created, giving the option of dining in the sun. A single planter running down one side of the garden is raised up in a bid to keep the majority of balls and other toys away from the plants.

DESIGNER Alastair Howe

ABOVE There really is no need to sacrifice comfort when sitting outdoors. The thick padded cushions on these robust metal chairs can easily be removed and taken inside in poor weather.

BELOW Hot tubs can be used in all weathers and in all climates, which makes them extremely versatile and suitable for most types of garden.

RIGHT Cushions and beanbags covered in brightly coloured, showerproof fabrics make ideal seating for children. They are also fun for adults and immediately introduce an air of informality.

ABOVE In a quiet corner, this hammock takes up very little floor space, and doesn't need conveniently placed trees as supports. Here, two blocks of wood secured in the ground do the job.

Rest and relaxation

Gardens are well known for their therapeutic, restorative properties, and while some of us may reap these benefits through the act of gardening itself, those less horticulturally minded may prefer to seek refuge in the arms of a comfortable chair. Owners of urban gardens often describe them as places of sanctuary – somewhere to escape from the rigours of daily life, to unwind and relax and maybe read the newspaper. There's no point having a garden if you aren't going to enjoy it, and to do this properly you have to have places to sit or even lie down. Choosing and positioning furniture for the garden requires just as much thought and consideration as selecting a sofa and other furniture for your living room.

RIGHT Curved seats are appealing to the eye but stone can be cold to sit on for any length of time. Cushions may be needed.

CREATING A GARDEN RETREAT

There are a few primeval desires that need to be satisfied before we can properly relax – it's a matter of basic psychology. Our most fundamental need is to feel safe and physically protected. One way of achieving this in the garden is to position the seating so that it is partially enclosed. Alternatively, you can arrange it so that you sit with your back up against something, such as a wall. You can take this a step further by adding some form of canopy or simple screening that will hide you from neighbours. We think of this as a need to create privacy but it really stems from a yearning to feel safe.

Probably the worst kind of seating scenario is to be perched on a raised, open-sided platform that feels like a stage; we are much happier lower down, surrounded by plants, screens or walls. This also gives protection from the elements, which again harks back to our needs as cave-dwellers.

You may also crave privacy from your own house. You might want to tuck yourself out of sight, away from the windows and from the intrusive noise of your own telephone. The trick is to identify a corner of the garden that is least overlooked, furthest from any noise source and also gives you a pleasant view.

CHECKLIST

WHAT KIND OF RETREAT?

- How much room do you have for furniture? ☐
- What sort of furniture do you want? ☐
- How many people do you need to allow for? ☐
- Do you need to improve your visual environment first? ☐
- Do you need extra storage? ☐
- Is the garden exposed? ☐

BELOW Although entirely open on one side, this garden structure, with a lattice roof for shade, offers a sense of privacy, thanks to the rear hedge and walls.

" Comfort is much more than having a soft cushion to sit on; it's about being in a well-designed space "

FOCUS ON FURNITURE

The furniture is, of course, paramount – there's no point picking an idyllic spot for your retreat and then sitting on an upturned crate. Think about what you want: comfy chair or lounger? Most loungers are over 2m (6½ft) long and you may simply not have enough room for as many as you'd like. Some of the more comfortable pieces of garden furniture on the market have solid weatherproof frames, which can be left outside year-round. The bulky cushions are generally showerproof, but during the wetter months they will need to be stored, preferably indoors. The space implications of this need to be considered before you go shopping.

ABOVE Designed exactly like a room, this garden has separate sitting and dining areas, and offers a choice between sun and shade.

LEFT While extremely comfortable, loungers take up a lot of space, so you may not be able to provide one for everyone.

Planning in close-up

- Consider whether you need to mask the noise of traffic or neighbours.

- Find a way to screen out neighbours and ugly views.

- Spend time choosing the right sort of furniture that caters for your comfort and lifestyle, as well as the size of your family.

- Minimize hassle by being organized and having enough storage: dragging furniture from the back of sheds and hunting for cushions is far from relaxing.

WHAT MATTERS TO YOU?

Look at how you like to relax in the garden. Will you be on your own, with a partner, or with an entire family and friends? You may even be with all of the above, depending on the occasion. Seating everyone comfortably may be impossible, and it may not be necessary anyway. Excessive seating will clutter up and spoil a small garden but the amount of space you have will be the deciding factor for the seating you choose. Hammocks take up little room but they aren't very sociable. Loungers, on the other hand, can be huge.

LOOKING AT LOCATION

The days of the week when you use the garden may be significant. There is likely to be less noise from traffic or local schools at weekends but more noise from lawnmowers and other households, which could affect the location of a seating area. You may want somewhere to sit on your own to have a quiet cup of coffee in the morning sun and then, later in the afternoon, lie on a lounger. If you want to read a book or a newspaper, you'll probably want to do so out of the glare of the sun. You'll need to study how the sun moves around the garden, thereby identifying areas of sun and shade.

If you intend to use the garden at night, think about lighting and heating. Outdoor heaters aren't ecologically sound and may not even be necessary. Some benefit can be obtained from walls and paving that soak up the sun's heat during the day and then give it out in the evening as they cool. Dark paving and walls absorb and radiate the most heat.

GOOD AND BAD NOISE

Nowadays noise is often thought of as a form of pollution, and with good reason. It is hard to relax when you are under a flight path, or next to a main road or noisy neighbours, but there are solutions. Water features can be used to mask sound. Even a gentle bubble fountain will take the edge off a nearby motorway, while a more dramatic cascade can help disguise the roar of a 747. The most important thing is to consider your neighbours, who may just add your lovely water feature to their list of noise pollutants.

As well as disguising offensive noise, moving water also generates negative ions. These cause the invigorating feeling you experience when taking a shower or standing next to a waterfall. To a lesser extent, they can be replicated by a garden water feature.

ABOVE It doesn't get much more relaxing than lying down in a hammock. Some can be objects of beauty and stunning focal points in their own right.

OPPOSITE Form often triumphs over function. When furniture looks great but is extremely uncomfortable, improve it with cushions.

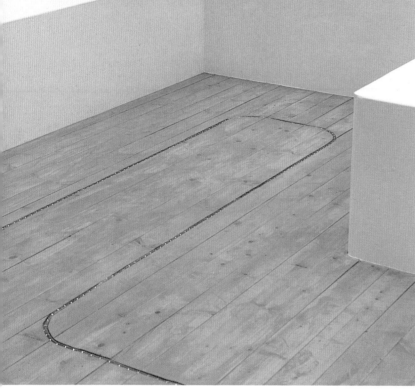

THE BIRDS AND THE BEES

The benefits of pet ownership are well documented: keeping animals can increase your sense of well-being and even make you live longer. In the garden, a similarly calming and therapeutic experience can be achieved by watching fish gliding around a pond or by encouraging various forms of wildlife to feed there. For many people, the presence of animals, even just a few sparrows on a bird table or squirrels in the tree, can be hugely relaxing. It's all about getting close to nature.

PLANTS FOR RELAXATION

Plants are the key to creating a relaxing garden environment. Green is at the centre of the

" The human brain perceives green as the most relaxing colour, which is why gardens and plants can be so calming "

ABOVE Solid painted concrete benches are part of the architecture of the garden and can look wonderful. However, for practical use, they are comfortable only with the correct soft furnishings.

RIGHT The mattress on this day bed has a showerproof cover, even though the whole thing is on wheels and can slide back into a weatherproof shelter.

OPPOSITE Scented plants are appreciated most in warm sheltered spaces, where their perfume can't drift away on the breeze.

colour spectrum, so the human brain perceives it effortlessly; it is also the predominant colour of nature and taps into our subconscious, bringing an air of tranquillity and reassurance. It follows that the most calming gardens are those that are mainly green, where there is an emphasis on foliage rather than flowers.

Vibrant hot colours, including reds and oranges, are energizing rather than restful, while cooler pastels and natural earthy colours are calming. Blue is particularly soothing, again because it is the colour of nature that we perceive in the sky and in water.

Dense planting can filter noise and, in urban areas, climbers on walls will deaden sound and prevent it from reverberating off buildings and becoming even more intrusive. Bamboos, grasses and trees, especially eucalyptus, will rustle in the faintest breeze. This in itself may be enough to cover up an irritating noise, but the mesmerizing effect of the sound and motion can also be deeply relaxing. Crying babies used to be placed in their prams beneath gently swaying trees to calm them down but, subliminally, this can also brighten the mood of an adult – the pram may not be necessary.

SHORT CUTS TO R & R

- Smell is an evocative and powerful sense. A sheltered spot can trap a scent but it must be soothing, not overpowering. Some people consider the scent of lilies, for example, too intoxicating, to the point of being unpleasant, like someone wearing too much cheap perfume.

- Harmony is the key to a relaxing garden. Don't go for a riot of colour but instead opt for a limited range of hues that complement each other.

- Soft pastel shades, greys and pale earthy tones are the most restful, whereas hot vibrant colours are invigorating and energizing.

- The gentle sound of grasses and bamboos rustling in the breeze, combined with the sight of their swaying motion, can really add to a restful atmosphere.

- Irritating noises from outside the garden can be masked with rustling plants or the soothing sounds of a water feature.

- Be careful with water features, however: a quietly bubbling fountain can be relaxing, while a roaring cascade is the complete opposite.

- Comfort is essential for rest and relaxation. Choose a warm, sunny spot that can be shaded when it becomes too hot, and provide shelter from the wind, if necessary.

- Make sure that your garden furniture is comfortable, otherwise you will never feel relaxed. Soft furnishings, particularly cushions, play a vital role in achieving this and shouldn't be underestimated.

- If you wish to read a book or newspaper outside during the daytime, you will need some kind of shade from the glare of the sun. At night, you will need suitable task lighting from above.

- Being on display is not relaxing, so screen out any overlooking windows, as well as any ugly views, to improve your outlook.

CASE STUDY: **Zen appeal**

ASPECT This garden, which measures roughly 15 x 16m (50 x 52ft), was formed when the architect merged two adjoining properties to create a single home for his clients. The plot drops away from the back of the house by over half a metre (about 20in).

BRIEF The couple wanted to create a home and garden that would be suitable for their grown-up children to visit with their own families. The interior is open-plan, clean and modern, and a smooth transition between the house and the built landscape was requested. It was important for the garden to complement the contemporary architecture of the house.

CONSIDERATIONS The budget was under pressure, with the original design concept deemed too expensive, so a strong but simple solution that would fit within the cost constraints was called for. The design had to be almost chameleon in nature: visually interesting from above, at ground level, during the day, during the night and in all seasons.

Birch trees are planted to screen the garden from neighbours. They add seasonal interest when the leaves turn in autumn and are underplanted with daffodils for the spring.

The simple planting palette relies mainly on bold blocks of white and green, which is incredibly relaxing.

By interlocking and overlapping all these parallel components, the garden hangs together with a very strong cohesive design, where each element interacts directly with its neighbour.

The structural linear concrete plinths can also be used as benches. They "widen" the garden, control movement through the space and introduce layers emphasized by the planting.

Fostering calm and a sense of well-being

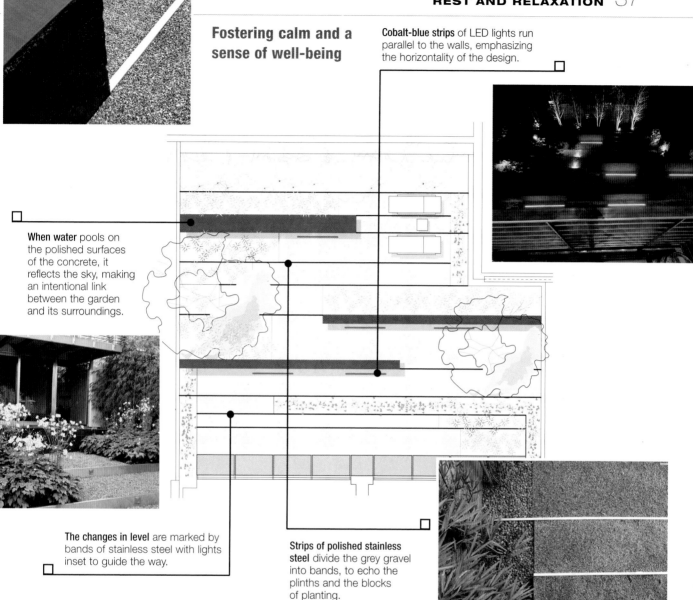

Cobalt-blue strips of LED lights run parallel to the walls, emphasizing the horizontality of the design.

When water pools on the polished surfaces of the concrete, it reflects the sky, making an intentional link between the garden and its surroundings.

The changes in level are marked by bands of stainless steel with lights inset to guide the way.

Strips of polished stainless steel divide the grey gravel into bands, to echo the plinths and the blocks of planting.

DESIGN SOLUTION Inspiration came from labyrinths, where purposeful walking is used to achieve a meditative state. This was translated into the garden by compelling the visitor to take an indirect path that is not dictated by the spatial boundaries.

Seen from above, the landscape is linear and highly graphic. However, as you enter the garden, the design unfolds gradually, encouraging exploration and movement, although with a calm, meditative quality. Freestanding walls built from black-coloured concrete slice across the space. These three-dimensional bands are echoed by the lower-level planting, with each bed containing a single species to increase the visual impact. The grey gravel surface is similarly subdivided into bands by strips of polished stainless

steel that span the width of the space and reflect the sky. At night, the linearity continues, with inserts of cobalt-blue lighting in the gravel.

This is a garden of strong contrasts, both in colour and in texture. Each element has been clearly defined and is distinct from its neighbour – even the concrete bands are roughened on the edges and polished on the tops. The simplicity of the garden brings with it an atmosphere that is immediately soothing, relaxing and contemplative. There is a definite Zen-like quality about it, while the gravel, black structures and bamboo also suggest a subtle influence from oriental gardens.

DESIGNER Andrea Cochran

ABOVE Home offices often end up in the garden because of a lack of space in the house, but that's no reason for them to be unsightly. The sedum roof on this structure is not only attractive but it also keeps the interior cool in summer and warm in winter.

BELOW The garden is the best place for this artist's studio, which receives plenty of natural light. Like Monet, this artist also has ample inspiration on his doorstep.

RIGHT Having a view from a home office window can be stimulating. However, if there is too much to look at, it can become a distraction.

ABOVE You may not need a space-age pod to use a laptop outside but you will have to shade the screen from the sun. A power socket could be quite useful.

Working

For some people, popping into the garden with a laptop is as close as they will ever get to working outside. However, more and more people work from home nowadays, and the garden may not be such a bad place to do it. You might need only a decent chair to sit in for making phone calls or perhaps a table to spread books out on, but if you are seriously committed to working from home, you could genuinely adapt your garden to become a highly productive workplace. Distractions can be something of a problem, and if you are a keen gardener, you could find yourself doing more deadheading than analyzing spreadsheets. Let's face it, everything else is far more interesting when you should be working.

RIGHT A quiet corner with some shade and shelter, a table and a chair may be all you need to do the occasional bit of work outside. This simple setup doesn't detract from the overall look of the garden in any way.

CASE STUDY: **Work and play**

ASPECT The rectangular garden is a flat plot measuring 23 x 10m (75 x 33ft), with the glass front of the home studio roughly facing the midday sun. The garden is open and sunny and surrounded by other gardens. Privacy is not an issue.

BRIEF An environment that was conducive to work – gently stimulating, without being distracting, and enjoyable for long periods of time – was requested. The studio building had to have a strong and dynamic connection to the garden space, as well as providing separate areas for informal al fresco meetings and work breaks. Importantly, the outdoor space should also function as a regular family garden, particularly at weekends and during the evenings. It should, therefore, not look like a work space.

CONSIDERATIONS It was necessary for the studio building to sit within the plot so that it connected to the garden both at the front and at the rear. The large glass windows and sliding doors with a level threshold were essential, so that even when they are closed in winter, there is an almost seamless division

The waterfall from the roof is almost entirely silent, as the water slides down a fine metal mesh. Its movement is stimulating, yet, because it is quiet, it isn't distracting.

Large glass doors slide right back, connecting the office space with the garden, while the planting behind the studio allows the building to integrate fully with the garden space.

The vibrant orange furniture pulls together similar but softer tones in the planting, wall sculpture and tree bark, and invigorates the garden, preventing the duskier tones from appearing sombre.

The green lawn contributes much to the overriding calm atmosphere. The adjacent bench allows people to get away from the immediate vicinity of the studio for breaks.

Mixing business and pleasure

Oak cubes form a sculptural path through the planting, connecting the lawn to the terrace, where they become occasional seats.

The voids set within the highly reflective pool are suitably thought provoking in a working environment.

At night after work, the interior studio lights reflect on the pool to create a stunning view from the house.

The colour palette is deliberately limited: a lot of colour would make for a potentially distracting and unsettling view.

between the interior work space and the garden. During the summer months, they slide right back to open up one wall of the building. The stone paving material of the terrace continues into the office. The intention is that when seated at your desk, surrounded by all the office amenities, you feel that you are within the garden.

DESIGN SOLUTION The floorplan of the garden is very simple, made up of a series of interlocking rectangles. This creates a strong framework on to which more intricate planting can be hung without the risk of the garden becoming cluttered and therefore disorderly and distracting. The rectangles themselves are rotated through approximately 45 degrees, which has the effect of making the garden seem wider and longer.

The inside of the office is painted white, a colour deemed by psychologists to be the best for encouraging productivity. Some warmer, richer colours have been injected with the triptych of sculptures mounted on the internal wall. Their red and orange tones are said to make for a friendlier and more invigorating workplace.

When used for their sculptural qualities, oak cubes can double up as seating for informal meetings. In this garden, they are positioned both inside and on the terrace, where they turn into an unusual pathway leading through the planting. Trees cast some shade on the terrace, which is ideal for anyone wanting to use a laptop outside.

DESIGNER Andy Sturgeon

Privacy

A garden that's overlooked and lacking privacy can be incredibly uninviting. It's vital to prevent this sort of situation early on or you could end up creating the most beautiful space but never using it because you can't relax and go about your business undisturbed. A feeling of enclosure is a deep-rooted human need, as it helps us to feel secure, safe and comfortable. But you don't want to feel as if you are in a prison; the trick is to get the balance right between an open garden that feels spacious and a partially enclosed garden that manages to be private.

LEFT A sense of privacy can be provided by canopies that block out neighbouring windows looking down on to your garden. The walls to the sides of this garden also hide the neighbours while keeping the view open.

LEFT Sitting right in among the planting automatically delivers a sense of privacy and intimacy. Even a single plant in a well-placed pot can enforce the feeling of enclosure.

ABOVE Slatted timber screens act like net curtains – they allow you to see through them when you are nearby, but otherwise they work almost as well as a solid screen.

BELOW Standard trees in small spaces can be successful: the canopy of leaves hides you from prying eyes, while the trunk need not take up much valuable space below. Decking can be taken fairly close to the trunk without risk of damage.

ABOVE In a narrow garden, tall arching plants right up against the seating area will very quickly enclose the garden, creating a buffer zone between you and your neighbours.

LEFT Pleached trees are clipped like a hedge on stilts, to provide screening high up without encroaching on valuable space at ground level.

Warning: what not to do

- Don't become obsessed and end up boxing yourself in – often just a suggestion of privacy is enough.

- Don't go crazy with pruning until you've decided what would be useful to keep. A mature bush or tree, which would take years to replace, could be invaluable.

- Don't be afraid to leave certain parts of the garden or views open.

- Don't bite off more than you can chew – you may need to make only a small part of the garden private, not the entire area.

BEING PRIVATE

It's relatively easy to make a garden or at least parts of a garden feel private, even if you live surrounded by hundreds of other people in the middle of a city. A well-placed canopy or a simple trellis on a fence may be all you need. But if you intend to use vegetation as the solution, it's important to identify the problem areas as early as possible to give the plants time to grow and get established. Built structures have the advantage of being fairly instant, but you shouldn't underestimate the usefulness of plants. Be careful not to chop anything down until you've had a good look at its merits. A bad mistake could leave you with a gaping hole.

CLEVER COMBINATIONS

To block an entire neighbouring building could mean planting a wall of trees and banishing the sun from your own backyard. But screening doesn't need to be only on the boundary – it can work well within the garden itself. By far the best approach is to go for a combination, perhaps a high fence along the perimeter and a small tree, even a screen, right next to the seating area. It also pays to be selective: a single tree between the seating area and a particular window that overlooks you may well be sufficient. Often it doesn't even matter if you don't achieve total privacy – it really is the thought that counts. What you should aim for is just a sense of privacy. If the neighbours want to peer at you through the trees, they will, whatever you do, but the chances are they won't, so placing a tree or a bush or a wall between you and them is probably enough. That way, you won't end up constantly facing each other over the fence when you aren't in the mood for a chat.

HOW IMPORTANT IS PRIVACY?

- Are there key areas where you're overlooked? ☐
- Will screening block out sunlight? ☐
- Does moving a seating area make it feel more private? ☐
- Do you need instant results or can you wait for plants to grow? ☐

SHORT CUTS TO PRIVACY

- Plants must be strategically placed. A bush right next to your chair may make you feel hidden from view, but if you were to place it 3m (10ft) away, it would need to be 10 times as big to achieve the same effect.

- Identifying the major offenders – specific windows that look on to you, low boundary walls, or just a general sense of exposure – and then tackling them accordingly, rather than trying to block out everything, may give you as much privacy as you need.

- Certain climbers will sit on top of a wall or fence, giving it vital extra height and making elaborate structures unnecessary. The quicker-growing ones will achieve good coverage within a couple of years.

ABOVE When seen face on, the solid timber columns allow views through them, but at an oblique angle, they offer significant privacy.

LEFT As they are severely overlooked, the owners here have created a slatted structure that admits plenty of light but turns its back on neighbouring buildings, while leaving the attractive views open.

CASE STUDY: **Urban seclusion**

ASPECT This compact space, measuring barely 5 x 5m
(16 x 16ft), is fairly typical of a small urban garden.
Sandwiched in between rows of back-to-back houses, it is
overlooked by countless windows, giving a real sense of
neighbours "living on top of each other". The garden faces
west but a mature tree in the adjacent plot blocks the light.
BRIEF The client asked for a garden that was suitable for small
dinner parties and provided a place to sit out and read in
solitude. Privacy was absolutely paramount and, because
there are large glass doors stretching the width of the house,
it was important to screen off the house opposite, which not
only looked on to the garden but right into the house itself.
At the same time, the large expanse of glass meant that the
owners' garden was on permanent display, so it became
equally important for it to look great even in winter.
CONSIDERATIONS Standard-height fences meant that chance
encounters with neighbours were always likely. Neighbouring
buildings at two and three storeys high could be screened

The flame-shaped canopy of the fastigiate
Carpinus betulus (hornbeam) provides
excellent screening above the boundary
height yet takes up little valuable floor space.

Lighting within the garden creates a mood of
intimacy but the sense of privacy is further
enhanced as it overpowers intrusive light
from adjacent buildings and other sources.

Some parts of the garden will inevitably feel
more private than others, so any furniture
has to be carefully sited and any screening
strategically positioned.

The lighter colour and warmer texture of the
strips of beach pebbles between the basalt
paving echo the linearity of the overall
design, unifying the space.

Providing maximum privacy

The stainless-steel water sculpture reflects light, introducing a greater feeling of space into this enclosed and private retreat.

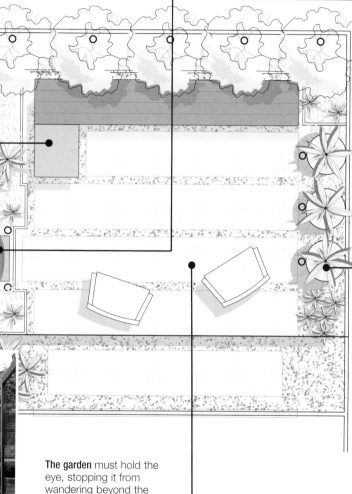

Good design plays subtle tricks: an L-shaped motif is repeated in the bench detailing and the planting beds to tie the design together.

A totally symmetrical design would have been too static. The row of sculptural pots along one boundary adds movement and dynamism.

The garden must hold the eye, stopping it from wandering beyond the boundaries, otherwise the sense of privacy will be lost.

ASPECT This compact space, measuring barely 5 x 5m (16 x 16ft), is fairly typical of a small urban garden. Sandwiched in between rows of back-to-back houses, it is overlooked by countless windows, giving a real sense of neighbours "living on top of each other". The garden faces west but a mature tree in the adjacent plot blocks the light.

BRIEF The client asked for a garden that was suitable for small dinner parties and provided a place to sit out and read in solitude. Privacy was absolutely paramount and, because there are large glass doors stretching the width of the house, it was important to screen off the house opposite, which not only looked on to the garden but right into the house itself.

At the same time, the large expanse of glass meant that the owners' garden was on permanent display, so it became equally important for it to look great even in winter.

CONSIDERATIONS Standard-height fences meant that chance encounters with neighbours were always likely. Neighbouring buildings at two and three storeys high could be screened only by planting, as built structures or over-high boundaries would fall foul of planning restrictions and might, in any case, enclose the garden in an undesirable way. The space taken up by the relatively large dining area resulted in only limited floor space for planting. Restricted access meant everything had to be brought through the house, preventing the use of

SOLUTIONS BY AREA

The design for a dark courtyard garden will be completely different from one for a garden perched on top of a building and exposed to the elements. The location of your garden will also dictate how you use it and, ultimately, your choice of plants, materials and even furniture.

ABOVE Get your priorities right. You can always eat and entertain indoors at the dining-room table and in the lounge, which keeps the balcony reserved for outdoor pursuits, such as sunbathing and relaxing in the hot tub.

BELOW The right sort of planting can be both ornamental and structural, offering privacy, screening and an attractive organic wind filter.

RIGHT A bistro-style table is just big enough to eat at, in which case you will need to make sure that the chairs are sufficiently comfortable to sit in for some time.

ABOVE This Japanese-style balcony blocks out the buildings in the foreground by using bamboo screening fixed to the inside of the existing parapet railings.

Balconies

A balcony is really just a small outdoor extension to an apartment. Often, it is neither a garden nor a room but merely the interphase between the indoors and the view beyond. In some cases, a balcony may be purely aesthetic and serve no practical purpose whatsoever, yet it can still be an invaluable piece of real estate. Rule number one is: don't expect your balcony to do too much. For many, the priority is simply to have a table and two chairs out there, and that's a sensible way of looking at it. Anything else should be seen as a bonus – there is nothing worse than cluttering up the entire space, making it unsightly and virtually unusable. When it comes to balconies, less is definitely more.

RIGHT A few simple trees protect the balcony and adjacent room from the sun and wind, and, at the same time, create a significant amount of privacy.

SPACE OR A LACK THEREOF

You'll need to take a good look at how you
intend to use this compact space because
the chances are there won't be a great deal
of it. "Space" is probably the key word here,
and some of the most successful balconies
are those that resist the temptation to fill
any empty gaps: a balcony crowded with
pots can appear as if the plants are about to
burst through the doors and into the room,
an effect that can be a little claustrophobic.

SCREENING VIEWS

Even if the view from your balcony is far from
spectacular, you will probably want to keep it
open – by leaving it unobstructed, you will be
bolting on to your apartment a feeling of light
and space that is difficult to put a value on.
Conversely, if the view is simply ugly, you will
probably be thinking about plants or some form
of screen to block it out. You may also need to
shield yourself from too much sunshine or to
filter winds and reduce eddy currents, which
can gust around balconies. But whatever you
do, don't wall yourself in. Make sure that light
can still penetrate to give you that all-important
connection with the outdoors and the sky.

ABOVE This design
draws heavily on
contemporary Japanese
styling. Minimalist in
approach, the balcony
is not functional but
sets a definite mood
and atmosphere.

LEFT Low-level planting
of mosses or creeping
succulents requires
virtually no soil, so there
are no weight issues.
The tree is treated like a
bonsai to keep it small.

OPPOSITE This unusual
backdrop provides
the division between
two apartments.
The apertures, some
including mirrors, create
the illusion of a greater
depth of space.

LOOKING LIGHT AND RIGHT

- Light is one of the most important assets of any balcony. Borrowed views of sky and skylines harness a colossal sense of space, and care should be taken not to obstruct this in any way.

- The connection with the outdoors is paramount, so consider the views not just from the balcony itself but from within the house or apartment.

- Choose materials and styles that reflect the interior of the adjacent room. This will create a flow from the inside out and vice versa, giving the illusion that both spaces are larger than they really are.

- The large doors and windows common in modern apartment blocks tend to frame balconies like a picture, helping them to look attractive from the outside. Apart from any practical use, balconies should also be designed to be appreciated from inside.

- Keeping things simple is the key to success. Develop a clear and concise plan and stick to it. Don't be tempted to fill the balcony with old, inappropriate pots and containers.

- Although they take up a very limited amount of space, walls and backdrops can contribute enormously to the finished design. Take your time deciding on the best way to treat them.

KEEPING IT PRIVATE

Your balcony should feel like an extension of the adjacent room, even when the doors and windows are closed. If you are overlooked by neighbours, the balcony could become a buffer zone, an area of plants or structures that shields you from prying eyes, even when you are inside the apartment.

Do go overboard with your balcony lighting. If you have an interesting cityscape to look at, too much lighting can overpower even the most jaw-dropping night-time panorama beyond. In addition, low-level lighting at night will enhance the open quality, especially if you can get away with not having blinds or curtains at the windows.

THE PLANTING DILEMMA

Plants dry out quickly on rooftops and balconies, thanks to their exposure to the sun and desiccating winds, but also because their roots are confined to containers and can't go searching for water. Many balconies don't have an outside tap installed and this has to be a major influence on which plants you choose, if any. Even if you are an avid gardener, the chances are you'll get a bit tired of filling up watering cans from the kitchen tap. You might then decide not to think of your balcony as a growing area at all, and instead opt for furniture or simple ornamentation.

Alternatively, if you simply can't be without plants, try to keep them to an absolute minimum – just one may be all that you need to provide that vital hint of green to keep you in touch with nature, even in the urban jungle. But regardless of how many plants you decide on, make sure you pick them carefully. Thick, waxy or glossy-leaved plants or those with

OPPOSITE Stunning views must obviously be preserved, but they can sometimes be improved with careful framing, using the right kind of plants and ornamentation.

LEFT Long, thin balconies are not very practical and should be zoned to make them as useful as possible. This could include space for seating and areas given over to planting.

ABOVE Simplicity is key. Pale walls and flooring reflect light, making this balcony seem much larger and brighter than it is in reality. The clipped topiary adds an architectural quality.

To plant or not to plant?

- Just a single plant can add a hint of green to a balcony, making it more welcoming and inviting, even on a grey day.

- Plants unsuited to balcony life will quickly start to look sick and unhappy. Choose wind-, sun- and drought-resistant plants from the outset.

- Plants are like pets – they need looking after, and someone will have to take care of them while you are on holiday. If you insist on having plants, see whether you can install an automatic watering system or, at least, a tap, to take the strain out of the gardening.

silver leaves are, for the most part, adapted to retain water, so usually make good choices. Bamboos, on the other hand, are particularly unsuitable because they are thirsty plants, and their thin leaves lose water faster than the roots can obtain it from the compost in the pot. Even if you are conscientious with the watering can, bamboos will still dry out very quickly. (For more on plants, *see* Rooftops, pages 58–65.)

CHECKLIST

WHAT DO YOU NEED?

- Comfortable chairs ☐
- Dining table ☐
- Enhanced view ☐
- Foreground interest ☐
- Plants ☐
- Privacy ☐
- Screening ☐
- Windbreak ☐
- Sun screen ☐
- Extension to room ☐
- Storage ☐

FURNITURE FACTS

- Bespoke, built-in furniture can be economical with space. Freestanding chairs, on the other hand, can get in the way and be difficult to squeeze past in a tight space.

- If the balcony leads off the dining room, there is probably no need to try to shoehorn a table and chairs into the balcony. Instead, dine inside with the doors and windows open, and opt for more comfortable and relaxing furniture outside.

- If space really is a problem, consider choosing lightweight, easily movable furniture for the interior. You can then take it outside whenever you fancy a change of scene.

- The quantity of furniture should reflect the number of people who live in the home – there's no point having only one chair for two people, for example.

- Weatherproof furniture is essential, but it should also be windproof, so that it's not easily blown over or, worse still, blown away. Flying chairs are a very real hazard!

- Your furniture may be virtually the only interesting feature you have space for on your balcony. Choose it wisely, as it will dictate the entire style of the design.

CASE STUDY: **A striking city balcony**

ASPECT This large balcony, about 12 x 8m (40 x 26ft), leads directly off the living room of a two-bedroom apartment on the third floor of a building. There is little shelter from sun, wind or rain. Most neighbouring buildings are sufficiently far away that the balcony does not feel overlooked, except on one side where the windows of a block of flats look directly on to it.

BRIEF The client wanted a bold, striking garden that was also simple and elegant. The priorities were to have an outdoor dining area and somewhere sheltered to sit. Since the space was to be used primarily at night, lighting was essential. A couple of fairly ugly buildings needed screening. Plants came quite low on the list of requests.

CONSIDERATIONS Because of the physical limitations of this balcony, and the regulations imposed by the owner of the entire building, the space could really only be accessorized rather than fundamentally altered. As with any balcony or roof garden, the load-bearing capacity had to be considered and, in this case, liaison with the developers and their

The combination of freestanding chairs and bench seating makes this space highly flexible. The bench also conceals the workings of the water feature and flambeau.

Bought off the shelf, the bottled-gas-powered flambeau is electrically controlled and ignited at the flick of a switch from a remote-control fob.

The simple bespoke bench allows the owner to sit in the warmth of the flambeau. Made from the same timber as the deck, it complements the bold simplicity of the design.

The hardwood deck quickly silvers in the sun's UV light. Regular oiling keeps it in condition, and the original colour can be brought back by pressure washing or with chemicals.

Making bold statements

The large picture window of the living room frames the balcony. The curtains can be left open because the apartment is not overlooked and, at night, the lights and flambeau turn the balcony into a piece of theatre.

An ugly railing, installed by the developer to protect a skylight, will soon be screened by the fast growing *Muehlenbeckia*, a twining evergreen climber.

The monolithic presence of the pool gives this balcony a real sense of drama. The black acrylic makes the shallow water highly reflective.

The combined bench and planter are made from a timber frame clad in cement board and then rendered and painted to match the existing parapet rail.

structural engineer showed that there was little capacity for additional weight on the roof. The parapet was already in place and, because the building uses modern construction techniques, the insulation layer was on the outside of the structure, meaning that nothing could be fixed into it. In effect, everything had to be freestanding.

DESIGN SOLUTION The existing, uninteresting, grey concrete paving had to be kept because it was part of the roof structure – removing it could potentially have damaged the waterproof membrane. Consequently, everything had to sit on top of the slabs. In order to make the space more dynamic, a hardwood deck, almost like an individual piece of furniture, was conceived. This introduced a change in level and masked some of the paving. It was kept away from the perimeters to preserve the 110cm (3½ft) tall parapet for safety reasons. The reflective pool was constructed from acrylic on a lightweight metal box-section frame. The water itself is only a few centimetres deep in order to keep the weight down, but the black acrylic makes the surface highly reflective, creating the illusion of depth. A gas flambeau was installed as a light and heat source, and also as a dramatic focal point that is reflected in the water. Sail fabric was used to make a canopy and, because it can be taken down, does not breach any planning regulations. A row of terrazzo planters containing *Nandina domestica* screens out the neighbouring flats.

DESIGNER Andy Sturgeon

Rooftops

In the past, rooftops were disregarded as unwanted or unusable spaces. Nowadays, their real value is widely recognized, and they present an opportunity to create truly unique and exciting spaces. For those with an eye on property values, roof gardens have become highly sought-after, in some cases quite literally adding an extra room – albeit one without a roof. These high-rise gardens are often visually dislocated from their surroundings, meaning that their design can be free from any burdening influence of adjacent architecture or distant views.

ABOVE This simple colour scheme repeats the use of white in pots, furniture, wall art and even the bark of the birch trees. The timber decking and lavender add warmth to the design.

ABOVE RIGHT Since a cubic metre (35cu.ft) of water weighs about a tonne, a hot tub is feasible only on a roof that's been strengthened for that specific purpose.

RIGHT Space is often so limited that the furniture is all that can be fitted in. Here, the planting has been restricted to the perimeter, providing privacy from above and below.

ABOVE Roof terraces are frequently seen from windows higher up and taller neighbouring buildings. This design is very graphic so that it works from above as well as from within.

LEFT Essentially, every plant on a roof garden is containerized and, where individual pots are used, they should be chosen with the same consideration as a piece of furniture.

THIS WAY OR THAT?

There are two approaches to designing a roof garden. The first is to accessorize the rooftop in much the same way as you would a room. The size and proportions are likely to be similar, and everything can be arranged more or less as it would be indoors. Furniture, containers, plants, sculpture, wall finishes and, to some extent, lighting all require virtually the same "interior" thought processes for the layout. This is an easy DIY or professional approach and can be hugely successful if well implemented, but if it is done badly, the results will look like a plain, flat roof with a few pots scattered around the edge, and a table and chairs in the middle. No heart and no soul.

The second approach is to overpower the geometry of the roof by introducing shape and structure. This allows much more scope for flair but, since this is likely to require bespoke planters and what amounts to minor building work, it can be considerably more expensive. The results, though, could be awesome.

LOGISTICS

How you access the roof will influence what you can take up there. Narrow stairs can be a problem, and you would be surprised at how many trips in a lift are needed just to get enough compost to fill planters. Vehicle-mounted hoists, usually used for furniture removals, are often the best solution, but major projects could even need a crane. The logistics of creating a roof garden are one of the factors that makes them so expensive – they often cost at least 50 per cent more than a similar space at ground level.

Planters, whether off the shelf or bespoke, often have to be placed around the perimeter, which can take greater weights. To present a coherent, uncluttered design, pots should be either all the same or at least from the same "family". Rectangular troughs and pots take up less space because they fit together and don't leave awkward gaps between them, which can collect leaves and other debris. Tall, narrow pots are useless because they blow over.

BELOW Palms, yuccas and agapanthus have thick waxy leaves that help to preserve moisture within the plants and combat the drying effects of the wind, which can brutally dessicate plants on exposed rooftops.

LEFT This windswept roof takes inspiration from the seaside for its timber decking and pebbled area, and for the plants with their thick waxy leaves, which makes them able to withstand the harsh conditions.

BELOW Steeply sloping roofs can be planted only if they employ a cellular system to hold the compost and plants in place. Water is fed in at the top and trickles down through each cell.

TECHNICAL NITTY-GRITTY

- Wind is a big deal. Plants and screening need to withstand the significant forces exerted on them. Everything, from pots to furniture, should be firmly anchored down or be of sufficient weight not to get blown away. Wind-permeable screens such as trellis are good at filtering wind.

- Planning and building regulations vary according to your location, so make sure you check these with your local authority. Particularly sensitive issues are the height of structures and trees, altering the look of the façade, and your roof being granted planning status as a garden.

- Balustrade and balcony rails should be 110cm (3½ft) high, with 10cm (4in) spacings between rails or bars so that children can't fall through them. Horizontal bars are frowned on because these are, in essence, an attractive ladder, and you'll never keep active children away from them.

- Any existing falls and drains should be preserved so that the roof's drainage continues to function in exactly the same way once the new roof garden is built over the top. For example, rainwater should pass through decking and be removed from the roof by existing drains.

- Weight is an important factor, even for a new, purpose-built roof. Obtain calculations from your architect or engage a structural engineer, who will tell you how much weight you can put on your roof and exactly where you can put it.

- To keep weight down, it is often necessary to make a special mix of compost, using 50 per cent peat-based compost, 20 per cent perlite and 30 per cent loam. Loam-based composts allow plant roots to anchor in properly and are heavier, giving pots a low centre of gravity, which makes them more stable.

LEFT Water features are a risk in all but the most sheltered of roof gardens. The wind can blast water out of the self-contained system and, ultimately, cause the pump to run dry.

PERFORMING PLANTS

Endeavouring to replicate a conventional planting scheme on a rooftop would be a disaster. Apart from the limited number of plant species that will survive in these very unique conditions, it is virtually impossible to achieve a look that is "gardenesque", where plants of different shapes and sizes can rub shoulders with each other in deep borders. The space and weight limits available for planting on a roof are likely to be relatively small and essentially container-based. This means there is no room for slackers. Every plant has to perform well, and often the best approach is to limit the number of different species and varieties you choose.

STARTING FROM SCRATCH

New planting should establish quickly, provided that you use fresh compost incorporating

Plant care know-how

- Automatic irrigation is vital to the success of a roof garden, so, where possible, install an outside tap with a simple battery-operated time clock.

- Repotting plants is difficult on a rooftop. The best way to do it is to scrape off the top layer of compost in spring and replace with new, or top-dress with a mulch of composted bark.

- Container-grown plants are both hungry and thirsty. Mix slow-release fertilizer granules into the top layer of compost in spring.

CHECKLIST

TOP ROOFTOP PERFORMERS

- Waxy leaves ☐
- Thick, succulent leaves ☐
- Silver leaves ☐
- Hairy leaves ☐
- Herbaceous perennials ☐
- Deciduous trees and shrubs ☐
- Maritime plants ☐

fertilizer and have good drainage at the base of the container in the form of a 10cm (4in) layer of very lightweight clay "gravel" (LECA). Automatic irrigation should supply exactly the right amount of water, while the heat that escapes from the building will gently warm the root zone. The provision of these virtually prime growing conditions could lead to plant growth at up to twice the normal rate.

MAKING YOUR SELECTION

The growing conditions on a roof are similar to those found by the seaside – often relatively warm but exposed to the drying effects of the wind. Bear this in mind when making your plant selection. If you opt for plants that succeed by the sea or originate from maritime areas, you can't go far wrong.

Other plants with special modifications to cut down water loss are also successful on rooftops. These include silver leaves, which reflect light; narrow or rolled leaves, which cut down water loss by having a reduced surface area; and thick, waxy or succulent leaves, which store water. Plants with spikes and thorns are best avoided for the simple reason that space is limited on a rooftop and it becomes difficult for people to avoid injuring themselves.

" The best rooftop gardens are a finely tuned balance of good design and engineering expertise, combined with extreme horticulture "

ABOVE A modern flat roof often includes concrete paving slabs, which hold down and protect the insulation beneath. These can be replaced with more decorative pebbles to fulfil the same function but without increasing the weight.

LEFT The lighting, sculpture, surface materials, furniture and pots are often more important than the actual plants in these unconventional gardens, which don't follow the normal garden design rules.

CASE STUDY: **A roof with a view**

ASPECT This penthouse has two roof terraces, one facing north, the other south, and both with commanding views. As they are 10 storeys up, the spaces are open and totally exposed to the elements. The majority of windows are on the north-facing side, where the terrace is shaded for much of the day by the building itself. To the south, there is nowhere to escape from the sun. Both terraces are exposed to the wind, which can be quite strong at times.

BRIEF A contemporary space was requested to complement the interior design and architecture of the building. The front, north-facing terrace has spectacular views to the edge of the city, which the client wanted preserved, while ugly office buildings in the foreground needed to be screened out. Shelter from the wind was essential. This narrow terrace had to be made more interesting with a defined living space separated from the adjacent bedrooms for privacy. The height of the handrail had to be retained at 110cm (3½ft), to comply with building regulations. This, though, imposed limitations on

Large evergreen shrubs on the south terrace provide year-round structure. They also introduce a feeling of privacy and screen out unsightly buildings and views.

To save space, a water feature has been incorporated into the low table. The glass top prevents the water from being blown around by the wind.

The hinged, curved seat is very welcoming and can accommodate one person or ten, depending on the occasion. The seat also provides storage beneath.

Even though interesting curves and organic shapes have been introduced, the weight is still predominantly distributed around the edge of the terrace, which can withstand a greater load.

Uniting two terraces

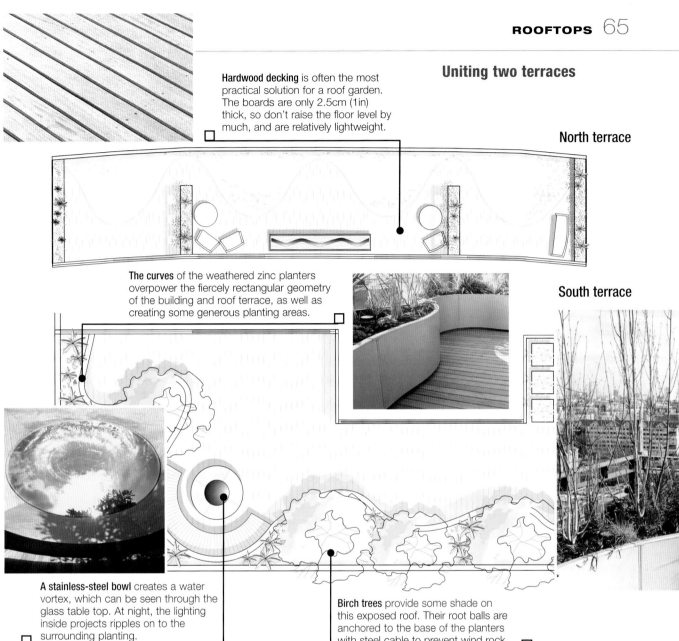

Hardwood decking is often the most practical solution for a roof garden. The boards are only 2.5cm (1in) thick, so don't raise the floor level by much, and are relatively lightweight.

North terrace

The curves of the weathered zinc planters overpower the fiercely rectangular geometry of the building and roof terrace, as well as creating some generous planting areas.

South terrace

A stainless-steel bowl creates a water vortex, which can be seen through the glass table top. At night, the lighting inside projects ripples on to the surrounding planting.

Birch trees provide some shade on this exposed roof. Their root balls are anchored to the base of the planters with steel cable to prevent wind rock.

the flooring choice, which could be only 5cm (2in) thick. There was no access to water on this terrace. The rear, south-facing terrace was intended for dining, with some storage space incorporated. A water feature was requested.

CONSIDERATIONS The architecture of the building, the handrails and window frames are the dominant features on this rooftop, and the proposed garden needed to complement these elements. The front terrace overlooks an international cricket ground, with views directly on to the pitch. In turn, large glass windows look on to both roof terraces, so the garden needed to have good structure and year-round planting. The load-bearing capacity was very limited, which meant that weight influenced every decision.

DESIGN SOLUTION Screens clad in weathered zinc are used like room dividers to create individual zones on the north terrace. Drought-tolerant planting in the top serves a dual purpose without eating into the overall space. Apertures within the screens filter the wind, slowing it down and lessening its impact without causing the eddy currents associated with solid barriers. These "windows" also frame views and allow glimpses of the garden beyond. Artificial grass flooring introduces curves into a potentially rigid rectangular scheme and injects some vibrant colour, which then connects visually with the cricket pitch below. This also overcomes the weight problems and lack of depth available for any new surfacing.

DESIGNER Andy Sturgeon

ABOVE The existing walls have been worked into a new design by incorporating bricks into the paving. The brick strips running from side to side also make this narrow space feel wider.

BELOW This courtyard garden runs directly off a kitchen/diner, where the mosaic tiling strip cuts into the internal flooring, linking the two spaces together. Planting is kept to a minimum in order to retain a large usable area.

RIGHT To maximize space, this platform with bench seating has been raised up and under-planted with ferns and other shade-tolerant plants. In this way, the beds don't eat into the restricted space of the lower terrace.

ABOVE Paving treatments are hugely important. Gravel, with its interesting texture, has a softening effect. It is a particularly useful material for more traditional designs.

Patios and courtyards

The hub of a garden is usually the patio: it's where you'll eat, entertain and congregate, and it deserves to be well designed because the entire garden can stand and fall on this one major element. Your garden could be so tiny that it consists of just a patio and not much else, something that we endearingly refer to as a courtyard garden – it's the sort of term an estate agent would use as it conjures up a notion of a cosy, romantic place. In reality, these diminutive, self-contained spaces can be used to create a very special atmosphere and are among the best of modern gardens.

RIGHT Making good use of the wall space, these hanging baskets are totally appropriate for a Mediterranean-style patio. Strategically placed pots underneath the baskets prevent people from walking into them.

DESIGNING THE SPACE

By their very nature, patios and courtyards are functional spaces, so first you must identify what you want from them. You might want to eat there and entertain, maybe have somewhere to grow a few herbs, perhaps include some storage and somewhere for the children to play. Measure the garden and draw it to scale on a piece of graph paper at, perhaps, 5cm (2in) equal to 1m (3ft). Then decide how much space is required for each of the various needs and draw circles to approximate roughly the designated areas.

Once you've done this, start refining the design and do more accurate calculations.

INTEGRATING THE PLANTING

The best approach is to design the patio so that the planting doesn't just feature all around the edges. Integrate beds, planting and other features, to bring life to large areas of uninterrupted paving.

Mean, narrow beds are pointless unless they are intended just for climbers. Other plants will spill over the edges and intrude on the space, so you may as well legislate for this early on by creating more generous beds. Make sure that the soil is deep enough for planting, and that the base of any paving, or the foundations of

CHECKLIST

DON'T FORGET

- Make the most of boundaries ☐
- Don't overfill the space with clutter ☐
- Get the balance right between planting and hard surfaces ☐
- Take care with your furniture selection ☐
- Avoid using too many different materials ☐

BELOW Recycling has been taken to extremes, with a crushed car forming the base of a table, and wine bottles used as a water feature and a gabion bench.

" The focus of any useful courtyard garden is likely to be the furniture, which has to be both practical and stylish. Get that wrong and you are sunk "

the house or of a wall, aren't lurking underneath. Don't skimp on this. If the plants don't have enough soil, they will struggle for survival.

Climbing plants are never successful in pots because they can't get enough water or nutrition. If you want to clothe a wall or fence, you will need to put the plant into the ground, even if it means breaking out concrete to create a bed. In tight spaces the balance between planting and hard surfacing needs to be finely tuned. Too few plants and an enclosed courtyard could be stark and uninviting whereas an excess of planting can make it seem cramped.

ABOVE With the same timber chosen for the decking, bench and table, this patio appears much larger than if a mix of materials had been used.

LEFT Black-stemmed bamboos stand out against the orange backdrop. The lower leaves have been stripped off to accentuate the colour contrast.

CURVES VERSUS RECTANGLES

Fundamentally, when it comes to designing your patio or courtyard, you have a choice of using either rectangles or curves. Highbrow designers will cringe at this simplistic idea of playing with shapes yet it's straightforward and it works. You may already be inclined to opt for one or the other but various factors may help you to decide.

Rectangular shapes – paving, planting beds, pools and so on – are likely to follow on from the geometry of your house and the shape of the plot. Rectangles are simple to use, as they fit into each other easily and can be overlapped and interlinked to make the design more interesting and dynamic.

Curves and circles can produce stunning results and even disguise the shape of a plot totally, making it seem bigger overall. They can also be incredibly economical with space – the apex of a curve can almost kiss the boundary, and where the curve swings back in again you can have a generous bed. Curves must be strong and flowing, not wimpy and apologetic, but beware: they are harder to design well and get right. They are also more expensive to implement: making curved walls, benches and floor slabs can add 25 per cent to the time needed for the project and, therefore, to the final bill.

MAXIMIZING THE BOUNDARIES

The boundaries are the most important ingredient of a patio or courtyard garden. You may wish to disguise them or highlight them. They can become a feature in their own right or be an attractive and interesting backdrop to plants and pots positioned in front.

New walls and fences can be costly, so rather than just erecting a boundary for privacy and security, think of it as a visual amenity as well.

Existing boundaries can also be improved. Unsightly or deteriorating walls can be painted or rendered. Old fences can be rejuvenated and painted black or dark brown so they recede, and plants and other features will then stand out against this foil. Shapes of plants become important particularly if they are backlit and silhouetted against them.

BLURRED DIVISIONS

It is common now to blur the division between inside and out. Doors with level thresholds make this easier to achieve but for simplicity the number of different surfacing materials should be limited, normally no more than three.

ABOVE The walls of the raised beds and pond have been clad in the same material as the paving to strengthen the bold design and provide plenty of occasional seating.

Flooring inside and out

- In reality, not many flooring materials are suitable for use both inside and out. Outdoors, exposed to the elements, many become slippery and potentially dangerous.

- Materials also weather differently inside and out – decking is a prime example. Although a popular candidate for outdoors, it does turn grey in sunlight over time, so it will never truly match an internal floor.

- Non-slip ceramic tiles are now available and are probably the only reliably inert product for use outdoors. As they are inert, they are not affected by sunlight, and therefore retain their colour.

- When continuing flooring from the inside to the outside, the best approach is to match the unit size and line up the slabs or tiles and run them in the same direction.

TRICKS OF THE TRADE

- If space is limited, make a raised bed dual-purpose by incorporating a bench seat or extending the top so that it is wide enough to sit on. This *in-situ* furniture then becomes part of the structure of the garden.

- Integrate the planting and the hard landscaping so that they interlock. Both these elements have to work together to ensure the overall success of the design.

- Using the same materials for your flooring and seating will give a cohesive unity to a design and also make the space feel bigger.

- Deciding on a colour scheme early on will give you a clear direction in which to work. Use a base palette of similar colours, for example creams, taupes and browns, then introduce an accent colour to warm things up.

- Think about the colour of everything – not just the paint on the walls and the flowers but also any stonework and, importantly, the leaves of plants, which play a huge role in the overall colour scheme.

- Never underestimate the versatility of plants. They can help provide privacy and a sense of enclosure, and also be used for shade, if necessary. Plants bring wildlife into the garden too.

- Some patios are sculptural in their own right. Walls, raised beds, built-in furniture and other elements should all work together.

- Restrict the number of different materials you use in a small space. Too many can be unsettling and also make the patio seem smaller than it really is.

ABOVE The circle of paving, the curved bench and adjacent wall make a strong sculptural statement in this secluded patio.

RIGHT The swooping curved wall encircles the patio, increasing the feeling of privacy and enclosure.

CASE STUDY: **A small but perfectly formed courtyard**

ASPECT This city courtyard garden, measuring around 4.2m (13½ft) wide by a little over 4.7m (15½ft) long, runs out from the kitchen of a terraced house. Facing south-east, the garden is overlooked from all directions.

BRIEF The interior of the clients' house had recently been refurbished in a very contemporary and fairly minimalist style, with white the predominant colour. The brief for the garden was that it should echo this approach. In addition, the garden had to be child-friendly – the clients have a young daughter – but it also needed to function as an adult space suitable for entertaining. Privacy was important and so, too, was the provision of shade. As the bi-folding glass doors open up the entire kitchen wall to the outdoors, the garden is very prominent year-round, so it needed to look good even in winter and especially at night. Lighting was paramount.

CONSIDERATIONS The real challenge was to make this very small space private without enclosing it too much, and to keep it feeling uncluttered and in tune with the interior.

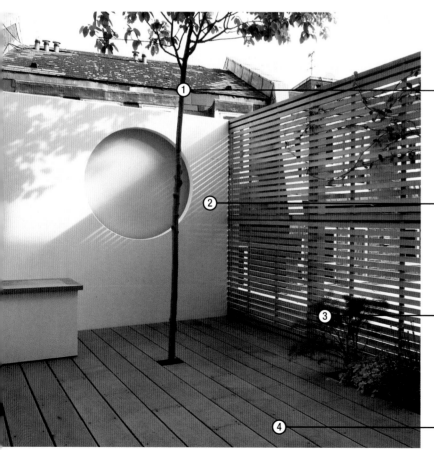

The snowy mespilus (*Amelanchier*) is the perfect tree for a small garden: slender, with spring flowers followed by fruit, which attracts birds, and then spectacular autumn colour.

Powder-coated stainless steel is incredibly durable as it is rust resistant and easy to clean. Using white in a small garden reflects the maximum amount of light, making the garden appear larger.

Even in this tiny space, there is still room for a few herbs, which can be very ornamental, especially if mixed with other plants.

Cedar decking boards are precisely the same width and run in the same direction as the flooring inside the house, making the garden feel like an extension of the kitchen.

Creating a private, modern haven

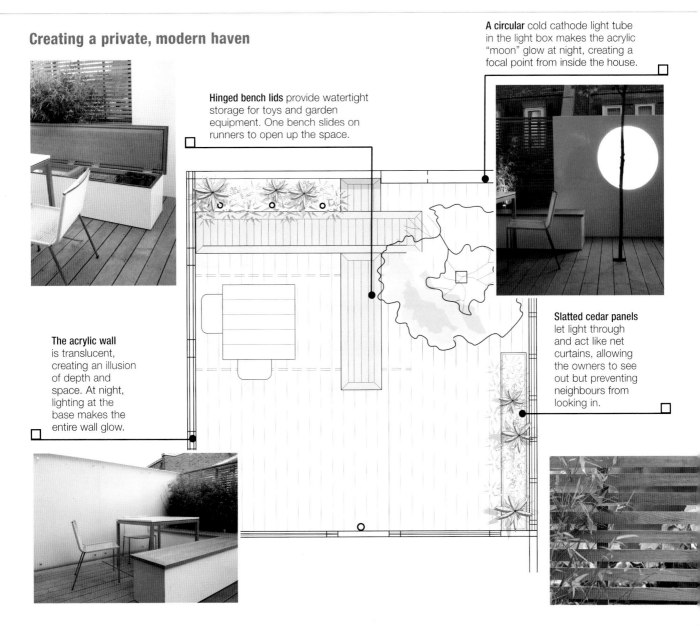

A circular cold cathode light tube in the light box makes the acrylic "moon" glow at night, creating a focal point from inside the house.

Hinged bench lids provide watertight storage for toys and garden equipment. One bench slides on runners to open up the space.

Slatted cedar panels let light through and act like net curtains, allowing the owners to see out but preventing neighbours from looking in.

The acrylic wall is translucent, creating an illusion of depth and space. At night, lighting at the base makes the entire wall glow.

DESIGN SOLUTION A small tree was planted in the decking to create shade for adults when dining and for children while playing. It also helps to reduce the temperature in the kitchen when the midday sunshine falls on the large glass doors. The tree gives privacy from neighbouring windows too. Two interlocking benches, coupled with a freestanding table and chairs, make a very flexible seating area. One bench on runners can be slid against the wall to open up the space to let children play.

The benches have hinged lids with waterproof seals and are used for storing childrens' outdoor toys, gardening tools and barbecue equipment. Installing a trap door in the decking

means that the void beneath can be used for storing large, bulkier items. The slatted timber screen, which runs around one and a half sides of the garden, allows light through and keeps a sense of openness in this tiny space, while at the same time maintaining privacy. One boundary is formed from acrylic sheets, backed by white powder-coated steel, with cold cathode strip lights at the base. The translucent quality of the acrylic gives an illusion of depth, making the garden feel less claustrophobic. A powder-coated steel light box forming part of another wall has a circular "moon" within it. When backlit at night, it glows a rich blue, transforming the garden completely.
DESIGNER Andy Sturgeon

ABOVE Often, basements and lightwells are appreciated primarily from above and from the sides, rather than being entered and enjoyed as a regular garden space.

BELOW If the steps down to a basement garden are wide enough, they will make the ideal spot for placing small pots and plants, which can then be appreciated at eye level as you ascend.

RIGHT Some lightwells are not intended as usable spaces. Rather they serve to let more light into the downstairs rooms, while providing a living picture to look out upon.

ABOVE Simple flooring creates an interesting textural tableau concealing a solid concrete base. A lack of soil means that all the planting is containerized.

Basements and lightwells

In old buildings, lightwells were thoroughly utilitarian areas and never considered things of beauty. They really existed only to let light into downstairs rooms. But the way we tend to live nowadays, with large old properties carved up into flats, these often tiny and awkward spaces are pressed into service as gardens. They still need to perform their original function of channelling light into the house – this alone is reason enough to brighten them up – but if a lightwell is the only outside space you have and all you can see when you look out of your windows, you should make the most of it. Subterranean living can be a little challenging at the best of times, but a basement garden will improve it no end.

RIGHT A lone tree can make a stunning centrepiece in a minimalist garden, but it is wise to choose a deciduous one so that it blocks very little light once the sun is at its lowest in winter.

GENERATING INTEREST

The temptation in a basement garden is to look skywards and seek the natural light; the design challenge is to keep the eye from wandering by giving it something to look at within that lower level. Furniture, containers or some other feature acting as a viewstopper will suffice. Interestingly, big things work best in small spaces, so a lone, dramatic pot will be far more effective than lots of little ones.

LIGHTING-UP TIME
Even though light-coloured stone paving or gravel used as flooring will help to maximize light levels, it is the walls that have the greatest effect, as they form the backdrop to everything.

" Light surfaces bounce natural light around, while dark materials are thieves of light and should be avoided "

ABOVE Water chutes are clever devices used here to link the upper terrace to the basement garden. The cascading sound is amplified by the enclosed space.

RIGHT Pale paving and white walls reflect the maximum amount of light into this narrow basement garden. Mirrors set in frames appear like windows and "double" the apparent space.

OPPOSITE These elegant, curved steps with open risers allow plenty of light through to the planting underneath, which makes good use of the limited space.

White or off-white walls reflect the most light but they also show dirt more readily, especially at the base where rain splashes back up off the paving or soil. However, if the walls are in a good state of repair, they are easily cleaned with a pressure washer. If you'd rather have a colour on the walls, go for something pale.

Think hard before painting a previously unpainted brick wall – once you start, there'll be no going back and you'll be repainting for ever more. Rendering a wall gives it a contemporary quality, but by smoothing over uneven brickwork, you'll miss out on the wonderful shadows it casts at night when lit from above or below.

Mirrors are excellent for bringing light down into a deep lightwell. Just ensure it's not easy to look straight into them, as this will shatter the illusion. A few millimetres of angle is usually enough to remedy this, but make sure you end up reflecting something attractive and not the dustbins or some other eyesore. Recessing or framing the mirror and hiding the edges with climbing plants gives the idea of a window and helps the illusion. Big is best; a whole wall of mirror can double the apparent space but if you don't keep them clean they will look dreadful.

LIGHT TRAPS

- In their favour, lightwells have something of a microclimate. They are well sheltered from wind and gain a little warmth from adjacent buildings. On the down side, natural light levels are reduced, which can restrict your planting palette.

- How the garden appears from above may be significant. The rosettes of ordinary ferns look particularly good, while tree ferns seem out of this world.

- A small tree may give you privacy from above but will exclude daylight from inside the rooms. Deciduous trees are best, as they are leafless in winter when light levels are low.

- A few architectural plants with large exotic leaves look better in confined spaces than lots of small-leaved plants – these have a tendency to appear cluttered and untidy.

- Don't be afraid to plant right up against the building. Provided there is sufficient damp-proofing, this shouldn't cause any problems.

- Variegated plants with golden or white parts to their leaves will bring light to dark corners. Variegated ivy is brilliant, although it can be a little rampant, and the varieties of the yellowy grass *Hakonechloa macra* are perfect.

- Be aware that anything planted above may steal the light from below. Also, once green climbing plants have covered all the walls, they are actually quite dark and suck up the light.

- On the whole, shady gardens make it hard to grow colourful flowering plants but, fortunately, many white-flowered plants will thrive, including *Libertia* and *Choisya*, whose blooms gleam in reduced light levels.

- Colour can be brought in with seasonal planting – busy lizzies will do surprisingly well in reduced light, and pelargoniums will thrive in the short term.

- Reflective pools can act like a horizontal mirror. A black-bottomed pool will reflect the sky and adjacent plants and harness daylight.

Going up the wall

- A painting, particularly a *trompe l'oeil*, or a motif on the wall will enhance the area without encroaching on the space.

- An ornamental water spout can be built into the wall for recirculating water into a basin beneath. The gentle sound it makes can help bring a gloomy area to life.

- Tall walls are an opportunity to mount lights high up. If sited correctly, they can mimic moonlight and create a magical effect.

- Space-saving trellis panels or wall art can be mounted at eye level and can be easily seen from indoors.

LEFT Pale materials will stop a basement garden from being dingy and gloomy. Light-coloured flooring needs regular cleaning to prevent it from becoming darker.

OPPOSITE LEFT There's no denying that white walls look incredible but there is a price to pay: they need repainting annually to retain their crisp and clean appearance.

IGNORE AT YOUR PERIL

Drainage has to be addressed. A badly drained subsoil, such as clay, could mean that plants will sit and rot in water; they may be better off in pots or in raised beds. Whatever surfacing you choose, it must drain, ideally into a storm-water drain or otherwise into a soakaway. Ensure that the exterior levels aren't higher than the damp-proof course in the walls or you could invite problems in the house.

AVOIDING TROUBLE

If access to the lightwell is difficult, such as through a window, this will influence how you maintain it. Evergreen shrubs need very little upkeep, perhaps only once a year. A spring tidy-up is best, when the plants can be fed, especially those in pots that would also benefit from a top-dressing with a few centimetres of mulch. Anything in pots will also need an automatic watering system, powered by a battery-operated time clock fixed to a tap. Otherwise, you could be climbing in and out of the window with a watering can.

Bare soil is a definite no-no since it will attract weeds, so make sure that your plants cover all the soil. A brilliant, though invasive, plant for this is mind-your-own-business (*Soleirolia soleirolii*), which will happily grow in shade and needs little or no soil.

Basements and lightwells adjoining a road tend to collect litter and other detritus from above. Planting at street level can act as a barrier to this but, inevitably, you will end up having to sweep fairly regularly. For this reason, it is best to avoid gravel flooring.

CHECKLIST

IMPROVING LIGHT LEVELS

- Paint walls white or off-white ☐
- Install a reflective pool ☐
- Use wall-mounted mirrors ☐
- Make the most of plants: for example, variegated leaves harness light, while white flowers gleam in reduced light ☐
- Use pale stone paving or gravel ☐
- Cut back overhanging planting ☐
- Avoid covering walls in plants ☐

BELOW Plenty of planting at different heights will take away the boxy quality of a small, high-walled space.

CASE STUDY: **A light and luxurious basement garden**

ASPECT The 5 x 4.5m (16 x 15ft) basement garden of this townhouse is south-facing, although the tall surrounding buildings throw it into shade for most of the day. Large glass doors lead out on to the subterranean courtyard from the living room, which lines one side of the garden. The remaining three sides are solid walls, which totally enclose the space, making it feel extremely small and dark.

BRIEF The idea was to create a colourful and luxurious garden that could be used day and night in summer and appreciated from indoors in winter. Artificial and natural light was to be introduced, and the walls had to be made less oppressive.

CONSIDERATIONS Access was through the house and involved lots of stairs and tight corners, so everything needed to be small enough and light enough to be carried through this route. Wind tends to eddy around the space, and this had to be overcome with some form of structure or planting. Parts of the garden had a solid concrete floor, which was too costly and time-consuming to excavate.

The walls have been kept free of climbing plants, as they would encroach on the space and conceal the reflective boundary treatments that bounce light into the garden.

The day bed, covered in weatherproof fabric, injects colour into the cool green space and makes an inviting focal point to the garden.

The glass shelf allows light through so that plants can grow underneath and none of the precious planting space is lost.

The inky pool acts like a mirror, harnessing light and reflecting the sky and passing clouds overhead. This, in turn, animates the garden and connects it to the surroundings.

Injecting light and colour

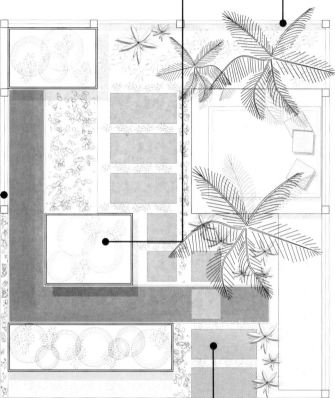

Big leaves in a small garden help to create a very strong and uncluttered design. The pale colours also brighten the space.

Translucent acrylic panels are backlit and at night give the illusion of windows leading to non-existent rooms beyond.

Water cascades down the louvres and gleams in even the faintest light. When the air is still, the motion of the water is particularly welcome.

Dark paving is non-slip and also masks any algal growth, which is more prevalent in basement and lightwell gardens that are deprived of natural light.

DESIGN SOLUTION Using alternating materials of different textures on the walls and including some that are translucent gives a depth to the boundaries, making the space feel bigger. The translucent acrylic panels, with louvres like Venetian blinds, are backlit. When illuminated at night, they give the impression of windows and hint at rooms beyond. Photographs of dry stone walls printed on to acrylic panels are a modern take on a *trompe l'oeil* painting and also reflect natural light. Real stone would have been too difficult to bring into the garden, and these ingenious *faux* panels don't take up valuable floor space.

Shade-tolerant foliage plants, including many evergreens, were introduced instead of flowering plants, which can be so fleeting. Foliage is more static and enduring, ensuring the garden looks good for a very long period. Golden foliage plants define a strong theme and bounce the natural light around, making the garden brighter. The canopies of tree ferns dull any winds that whip around the garden and also provide privacy from above.

The striking red colour in the fabrics adds warmth to a garden that rarely sees sunlight. This colour is echoed in the purple and red foliage plants and repeated in the powder-coated steel containers. These planters were introduced where the concrete floor prevented planting directly into the ground and were integrated into the overall lush planting scheme.
DESIGNER Kate Gould

Entrances and passageways

We tend to focus so much on our private sanctuaries – the garden hidden out the back – that we often overlook the approach to the front door, the space that takes you from street to house. Just as important, it gives the visitor their first impression, a taster of what is to come, of what can be found behind the door and beyond. It should be welcoming and say something about the person who lives there, but it is also a route that you probably take yourself every single day, so it makes sense to pay it some special attention.

LEFT An apron of contrasting paving or a step to the front door helps to define the entrance clearly, as well as enhancing the architecture of the building itself.

LEFT The approach to this modern house echoes the bold and uncompromising architecture. The planting on the left balances the timber structure to the right, channelling visitors directly to the front door.

ABOVE Less-trodden passageways can be improved with strips of creeping plants. Thyme and chamomile are able to withstand occasional foot traffic and will emit wonderful aromas when lightly bruised underfoot.

BELOW This courtyard acts almost as an antechamber – strong, simple and uncluttered, perhaps a precursor to the more important house beyond.

ABOVE Painting the front door in a contrasting colour and framing it with planting or pots is particularly useful on a flat-fronted building, where the front door doesn't otherwise stand out.

LEFT Even a relatively small front garden can accommodate a parking space without compromising the overall design.

Welcoming the right people

- Frame the front door with planting or pots to make the entrance more obvious for first-time visitors, and also more welcoming.

- Wide paths are inviting and less likely to have plants spilling out on to them from the borders – sharing a path with rain-sodden plants that make you wet when you brush past them is an unpleasant experience.

- Bear in mind that gardens hidden from view by tall hedges, fences and walls are a magnet for burglars.

EXTENDING A WELCOME

A front garden, no matter how microscopic, can be used to improve the appearance of a house; even a single plant can transform a drab façade. But while the mood should be welcoming, there are also practical considerations: the house number needs to be clearly displayed, and a porch might be required to shade people from the sun or from the rain while they are putting their key in the lock or saying their long goodbyes.

HOMECOMING

There should be a sense of arrival and, frequently, this can be achieved simply by emphasizing the front door. Where there's more than one exterior door, it's sometimes hard for a first-time visitor to know for certain which one they are meant to use and, far from being welcoming, this can be confusing and uninviting.

The problem can usually be resolved easily by "signposting" the route with the surfacing treatment, thus steering people towards the correct door. For example, you could create an obvious path in a particular stone, or make more of the front door by framing it with planting. The most basic solution is an apron of paving in front of the door and a pot on either side.

Paths to front doors are tricky. People can be lazy and will cut corners whenever they can, so you have to provide a reasonably direct route. If the path meanders too much, shortcuts will be taken – planting may be stepped over and a new path worn through a border.

Paths also need to be wide enough to be welcoming – narrow ones are not, and if rain-soaked plants encroach on the path, you have to fight them off Indiana Jones-style to reach the door without getting drenched.

MAKING AN ENTRANCE

- Is it obvious how to reach the front door? ☐
- Is the entrance welcoming? ☐
- Is the journey to the door hazardous? ☐
- Do you need lighting? ☐
- Is the house number obvious? ☐
- Do you need shelter from sun and rain? ☐
- Are there any burglar deterrents? ☐

BEING IN THE KNOW

- Scent plays a vital role in the front garden, appealing to the most evocative sense. Even faintly scented plants positioned by the front door can subliminally deliver the warmest of welcomes.

- A good structure of mainly evergreen shrubs is important because the entrance is likely to be used every day and should, therefore, look good year-round.

- If the design relies on flowering plants rather than just foliage, it is best to avoid species that flower only fleetingly. Where possible, choose plants that also have interesting foliage and fruit.

- Feng shui, if you believe in that sort of thing, dictates that a straight path to the front door is bad – a poisoned arrow aimed at the house. A gentle wiggle or an indirect route will resolve this.

- Gates are often the very first thing to be seen when arriving at the front of a building. They can also frame views and offer enticing glimpses of what lies beyond.

- The entrance to a home is the marriage between architecture and garden – one should always enhance and complement the other.

- Surfacing should harmonize with the building and can be used to reflect the architecture. Using brick paving to match the brick of the house presents a unified, holistic entrance.

- The approach to the garden from the house should also be addressed. Glazed doors will frame the garden like a picture.

ABOVE A simple flight of entrance steps can become quite striking with the addition of some carefully selected and positioned ornamentation.

LEFT Catching a glimpse of a garden that is framed by a doorway or gate is incredibly enticing, especially if it's private and you aren't allowed to enter.

BENEATH YOUR FEET

Since it will be used in all weathers, surfacing must be non-slip and firm underfoot. In wetter climates, this rules out timber decking and most ceramic tiles, which can be too slippery. Gravel can look great, is cheap and is considered a burglar deterrent, thanks to the crunching sound it makes underfoot. However, loose gravel can get brought into the house on the soles of shoes. One solution is an apron of paving immediately outside the door, which allows for a few strides and the gravel to be shed from shoes before entering the house.

SQUEEZING IN PLANTS

Giving an entire front garden over to paving can look terrible but, sadly, this practice is becoming increasingly common in towns where parking is difficult and expensive. It ruins the entire streetscape to the point where, if the majority of front gardens are paved over, house prices are actually driven down. An excess of impermeable paving also raises local temperatures, and flash floods are made worse by the run-off.

There are ways to get around this. Squeezing a few climbers in at the boundary edges can improve things greatly, and a lollipop-shaped tree will take up very little room at ground level. If you have only enough space to drive your car straight in and reverse straight out again, low creeping plants in the soil between where the wheels pass might be the solution. If you use the car a lot, think about creeping thymes and other sun-lovers, but if the car mostly sits on the drive, low-growing ferns and other shady plants might be a better option.

High front walls and fences are imposing and potentially intimidating. They give privacy but

OPPOSITE With the addition of just a few plants and ornaments, even a narrow passageway can be transformed into an atmospheric garden.

LEFT It's important not to overlook the appearance of the entrance into the front garden from the house. This doorway frames the view, while the linear surfacing draws people on.

ABOVE This brightly coloured façade, framed by two tall pots, makes a very clear destination for first-time visitors.

Good things to know

- Narrow passageways can be instant vistas, with a simple focal point at either end making all the difference: a sculpture or a carefully positioned pot will draw people towards it.

- Paved or concreted passageways, especially shady ones, are good places to have containers. The lack of sun means plants won't dry out and therefore need less watering.

- There is nothing more enticing and alluring than a glimpse down a passageway through a gateway and into an enclosed courtyard. The garden at the end can seem like a magical oasis.

also offer burglars cover, so a more open front garden that neighbours can see into is usually advocated by police. A good compromise is to plant both tall and low shrubs rather than a solid hedge. The garden will then seem reasonably open but the taller plants will stop passers-by from having a good nose unless they have no shame and stand and peer through the gaps.

Lighting has three roles: safety, security and aesthetics. The path can be illuminated at low level so people can see where they are putting their feet, and the front door can be lit to show visitors their goal. Remember that first-time visitors won't be familiar with potential hazards such as steps: illuminate these. Motion sensors or PIRs (passive infrared sensors) are useful, saving on energy and also deterring intruders.

" A well-designed and looked-after front garden not only improves the look of your own house but can contribute to the entire neighbourhood "

WIDENING YOUR HORIZONS

- Although passages between buildings are usually draughty and unappealing, making them the obvious place for storing dustbins and other unsightly objects, they can be used in a more positive way to increase the overall sense of space in a small garden.

- Pay attention to the surfacing: strips of brick or other contrasting paving draw the eye from side to side, creating the illusion of breadth.

- Wind is often channelled down passageways, creating something of a wind tunnel. Tall shrubs at one or both ends will filter the wind, reducing its power.

- Pale or white walls will reflect light, making a passageway more inviting. A light-coloured surfacing material such as gravel will also lighten the space, while wall-mounted mirrors can make the passage appear wider.

- Where windows look on to the side of a passageway, climbing plants and lighting, to brighten the area and wash the wall with light, will improve the view from inside.

- Smaller properties tend to have distinct front and back gardens with a passageway linking the two. Where security is an issue, lightweight trellis above a gate can be impossible to climb and will deter burglars.

- A passageway between two tall buildings can be claustrophobic and unsettling, like being stuck at the bottom of a crevasse. Put things on a more human scale by installing a false "ceiling" of plants and horizontal timber beams just above head height.

CASE STUDY: **An imposing, water-lined courtyard**

ASPECT The small courtyard, measuring 9 x 3m (30 x 10ft), forms the approach to the house from the street. It is almost completely enclosed by the walls of the building, although a short open section allows it to remain reasonably light and sunny. It is a private space, completely hidden from view by a wall and a solid gate.

BRIEF A visually uncomplicated entrance garden leading directly to the front door was required here. The atmosphere needed to be welcoming yet vaguely imposing, so as not to encourage visitors to linger – the space had to function primarily as a transition zone between house and street. A strong sense of arrival befitting the scale and proportion of the house was desired.

CONSIDERATIONS The space was not perceived as a garden in the conventional sense, but as it was neither garden nor house, there was a risk that it would end up feeling like a

The hard surfaces are carefully chosen to harmonize with the existing and highly visible copper roof of the house.

Welcoming figurative sculptures frame the front door, emphasizing the "goal" and drawing visitors along the path.

The boundaries of the courtyard are completed by a "wall" of bamboo, which casts shadows on to the paths and water surface.

In warm weather, the submerged path can be walked along barefoot, to provide an entirely different sensory experience.

Knowing that you've arrived

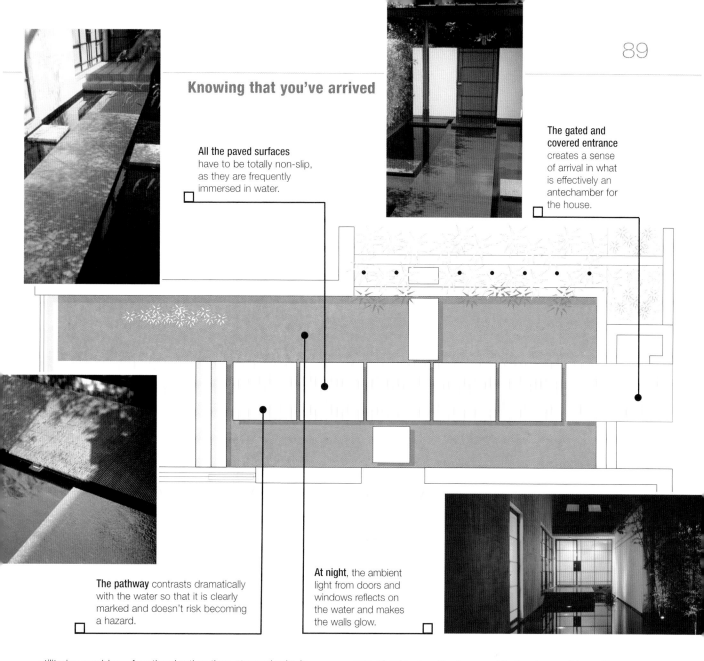

All the paved surfaces have to be totally non-slip, as they are frequently immersed in water.

The gated and covered entrance creates a sense of arrival in what is effectively an antechamber for the house.

The pathway contrasts dramatically with the water so that it is clearly marked and doesn't risk becoming a hazard.

At night, the ambient light from doors and windows reflects on the water and makes the walls glow.

utilitarian corridor – functional rather than atmospheric. It was clear that the architectural style of the building would always dominate this narrow space, with the various walls and doors all around suggesting that it was perhaps more of a room than a garden. The door and window frames have an unmistakable Japanese quality. Although not a pastiche, they do bestow a certain atmosphere or design direction upon the garden.

DESIGN SOLUTION The entire area is sunken down to create a wall-to-wall pool with a broad path spanning the water like a bridge or boardwalk. The floorplan of this space is strongly rectilinear, taking its cue from the geometry of the buildings that wrap around it and dominate the courtyard. The materials selected are from a simple palette of warm

natural colours, with stone and timber harmonizing with the copper roof of the house entrance.

The water used in the design is symbolic, intended to evoke thoughts of a moated castle and, perhaps, implying a physical barrier to deter intruders. In a unique and humorous twist that takes this historical metaphor even further, the courtyard can be partially flooded. The water level is able to rise just a few centimetres to cover the pathway, leaving only the steps to the house exposed. When submerged, the garden becomes even more intriguing and takes on an extra dimension: the shapes, colours and patterns of the paths remain visible just beneath the surface and are picked out by the sun, which gives them a warm glow.

DESIGNER Terragram

DESIGN DETAILS

Once you have the bigger picture clear in your head, you can turn your attention to all the specific ingredients that will make up your garden. These are the hard and soft materials that must be blended into the mix. Think of them as tools, with their level of importance varying depending on your individual needs.

ABOVE A limited colour palette of blues, silvers, greens and yellows from the same segment of the colour wheel delivers a cohesive look.

BELOW The flowers and foliage of these plants harmonize with each other, while the trunk of the multistem tree makes a direct visual link to the timber boundary walls.

RIGHT Planting in defined blocks, with strong contrasts of form, colour and texture, creates a planting style that is at home in either traditional or modern schemes.

ABOVE Extensive herbaceous borders are ideal for flower lovers but they can be a lot of work and leave little interest in the winter.

Planting design

For many people, plants are paramount and possibly the main point of a garden. However, they should really be thought of only as another exciting material – simply an extra tool to play with. Essentially, plants should be used to mould space and to create a mood or an atmosphere, something that they can do very well and very quickly. But, they have many other attributes, such as hiding walls, providing scent and colour, attracting wildlife or just uniting a scheme. The range of planting styles is huge and the choice of plants can be mind-boggling to the uninitiated. One of the best approaches is to find a style you like and then to copy it shamelessly, although there are still a few rules you need to follow.

RIGHT This garden proves that flowers aren't essential. It depends on different leaf colours and textures, with various greens enlivened by a hint of grey and a dash of purple.

CREATING THE PLANTING

Early on in the planting design process, the plants should be thought of in only broad terms, such as bulk and shapes rather than individual species or colours – that sort of detail can come right at the end.

Designers love to talk of mass and void. The plants are the positive mass – the bulk – with negative voids or spaces in between. These two elements should be in proportion: too little planting with huge areas in between can be soulless; too much planting can be claustrophobic and cluttered. It's a bit like arranging furniture in a room; the space you leave in between is every bit as important as the furniture itself.

TIME, THE FOURTH DIMENSION

Try to retain some of the existing planting – but only if it's appropriate to your new scheme – as this will give the new garden instant maturity.

A new garden should be planted so it looks okay almost straight away, quite good in three years and really excellent in five. As things grow, the garden changes, shade appears, some plants thrive, some don't. Keep an eye on your original vision, and don't be afraid to replant or replace certain plants to keep things on track.

BUILDING UP LAYERS

The planting should always be built up in layers. The first key plant in a small garden might be a solitary tree or a shrub, while in larger spaces you may have a number of these star plants to draw the eye, demand attention or dictate the overall atmosphere of the place. They tend to have a sculptural form and are often quite striking to look at.

Next, you build the skeleton or framework. This is usually the shrubs that give the garden and the planting its shape. They mould the space and can even overpower the geometry of the site; they screen and shelter, divide and define. Although some may have flowers, think of them only as shapes at this point.

And then there's the froth: perennials and bulbs, grasses and ferns that put flesh on to the bones of the shrubs, that give the planting most of its character, its colour and texture, and bring the garden to life.

OPPOSITE ABOVE After the flowers have bloomed, this garden retains year-round structure, which is provided by neatly clipped shrubs and hedging.

OPPOSITE BELOW Planting in well-defined blocks or drifts emphasizes the contrast between different plant varieties. Repeating a limited number of varieties makes for a strong, eyecatching design.

ABOVE By choosing a simple colour theme you automatically focus your ideas, making it easy to plant a garden with high impact, although such a restricted palette can become monotonous.

COMPILING YOUR PLANT LIST

You will need a list to work from, preferably a fairly short list. The best planting schemes are relatively simple, so it is essential not to try to cram too much in. It's a bit like packing for a holiday: the temptation is to take a lot of stuff that you don't need. And so it is with plants.

Knowledge of too many plants can actually be a hindrance; the skill comes in the editing. Draw up your list and then cut it at least in half. Be ruthless, because too many different plants will make an incoherent jumble, not a well-thought-out space.

Style, mood and atmosphere

Although the architecture of the space and the character of the site will heavily influence the eventual look of the garden, in all but the most minimal designs it is likely that the plants will ultimately define it. You should develop a clear style or mood for the garden. This may be based on a subtle colour scheme or could be a more obvious style, for example Japanese, but over-the-top themes, such as a seaside garden that's not by the sea, can be Disneyesque and vulgar and are best avoided.

ARCHITECTURAL

ABOVE The word "architectural" has come to be used for a range of plants that have a strong outline and a bold presence. Likely contenders may be palm trees, cacti and ferns. Foliage and form predominate, while flower colour is often irrelevant. This type of planting sits comfortably with modern residential architecture and could as easily convey the atmosphere of a desert as it does of a jungle.

EDIBLE

LEFT Wherever you live, keeping in touch with nature by growing a token amount of your own foodstuff may be important for your well-being. Herbs and fruit can also be ornamental, which is important when you have only limited space. Productive plants can be restricted to containers or mixed in among the other planting.

COLOUR

RIGHT A limited colour palette can make for striking results. Pastel flower shades can be romantic, while green and bronze foliage teamed with white flowers can seem daring and bold. Flower and foliage can also be linked to materials that perhaps harmonize with paint finishes on walls or echo the muted colours in natural stone paving.

STRUCTURAL

BELOW Plants can become part of the architecture of the garden: a hedge, which is in effect a living wall, is an obvious example. Even deciduous hedges provide structure in winter and can create a framework on to which everything else hangs. Blocks of ornamental grasses, pleached hedges, a row of one single tree species or a table of clipped yew can all become part of the structure.

NATURALISTIC

ABOVE This is hard to pull off in a small space. Its very essence is to mimic nature, which is usually on a larger scale. Mini meadows, woodlands and prairies may look good in books and magazines, but naturalistic plantings often have a peak that may last only a few months, followed by too much downtime for a small garden.

GRAVEL

BELOW Gravel immediately conjures up Mediterranean or arid climates, and the right planting can really emphasize this. A succulent, a palm or even grasses can be the starting point for a strong theme. The gravel allows light and space around plants, shows them off to their full potential and allows access for maintenance.

Key locations

Your choice of plants will be dictated by the location of your garden. Geographically, you will need to understand your climate zone; regionally, you may need to look at prevailing winds or soil types; and locally, you should look at sun and shade. Some small gardens are enclosed and may tend towards a microclimate. Roof gardens, on the other hand, may be unbelievably exposed. All of these factors will have an enormous influence on your choice of plant material.

WOODLAND

ABOVE Making the most of the shade, this contemporary take on a woodland garden includes trees ferns for structure, with the understorey mainly green foliage plants. These thrive in the lower light levels and create a very tranquil atmosphere.

SUNNY

LEFT The greatest variety of plants can be grown in the sun, and it allows flowering plants, in particular, to perform their best. The gravel mulch retains moisture in the soil and reduces weeding and watering, allowing plants to deal with extremes of weather.

FORMAL

RIGHT The neatly clipped blocks of evergreens introduce a structured geometry to the planting, which echoes the hard landscaping and accentuates the formality. The repetition of plants strengthens the theme.

EXPOSED

ABOVE Gardens without any shelter, particularly those by the sea, which are battered by salt-laden winds, have to rely on specially adapted plants like succulents and grasses with thick waxy leaves, and grey or hairy leaf surfaces.

ROOF

BELOW On a roof garden, plants will suffer from extreme exposure to sun and winds, much as in a coastal garden. Since plants will be in containers with only limited soil, they will dry out fast, so need to be drought resistant.

RIGHT Fibre-optic lights, encapsulated by glass, turn a conventional table into a sublime piece of intriguing sculpture – part furniture, part art installation.

CENTRE RIGHT Back-lit by spotlights, these monoliths of sand-blasted, toughened glass glow at night. The silhouettes of bamboo leaves are projected on to the glass, animating the garden in the breeze.

BELOW RIGHT The white bark of birch trees is highly reflective and easily picked out by a spotlight at the base. A light on either side of the tree produces a dramatic effect, even in winter.

Lighting

Lighting is perhaps the most important weapon in your design arsenal – at the flick of a switch, you can transform an ordinary garden into a magical wonderland. At night, the garden looks very different, and artificial lighting can pick out shapes, distort colours and add a touch of drama, which may be missing during the day. Lighting allows you to use the garden in the evening and into the night, and if you have a busy lifestyle, this could be when you go into the garden most often. It's hard to imagine a great garden without lights.

ABOVE Individual spotlights on spikes are concealed by a low wall. They uplight the small trees, bouncing light back down on to the paving and the dining area.

LEFT Art in the garden needs to be well lit, just as it does in the house. Sculpture like this casts interesting shadows, which contrast with the well-illuminated parts of the garden.

ILLUMINATING IDEAS

You need to think carefully about what you want to achieve with garden lights. There may be key features you'd like to illuminate – perhaps a wall or a tree? Do you need task lighting to read a book at dusk or eat out after dark, or do you simply want the garden to look good from indoors?

You may wish to increase the security of your home and use outside lighting to deter unwanted visitors. Infrared or motion sensors are ideal, but they can also be fitted for safety and practical reasons, such as to automatically illuminate paths, steps or even shed doors that you want to be able to see only when you are opening or closing them.

THE PERFECT FITTING

The most popular garden lights on offer today are low-voltage halogens. Available in a huge range of fittings, they provide a clean, white light and run off transformers. This means that they are safe to use in ponds, and if you do manage to cut through the cable accidentally, you won't get electrocuted.

LED fittings are improving all the time, and they are now bright enough to compete with halogens. They have an almost infinite lamp life, so you're never likely to have to replace them, and they consume only a fraction of the energy of traditional lights. They come in a range of colours; some fittings can even change colour at the touch of a button.

Fibre-optics can create amazing effects, from pinpoints of light to washing entire walls. Although more expensive to install, these lights are relatively low-maintenance because they have a remote light source.

Neon and cold cathode lights are useful for concealed strip lighting for the base of walls and underneath benches.

There are no installation costs involved with solar-powered lights, which can be positioned

LEFT Side-emitting fibre optics or LED "rope" lights come in a range of colours and can be used to pick out steps, pool edges and other garden details.

anywhere. On the downside, they never become very bright and the light doesn't last that long.

MOOD LIGHTING

Flexibility is the key to successful lighting. Install the fittings on a number of circuits so you can choose how many lights to have on at any one time and create a range of different moods. Each circuit can be for a separate part of the garden or a different "layer" or function of light, meaning that you can start with quite a subtle effect and build up to something far more dramatic. Even in a tiny garden, a couple of different circuits are worthwhile. There should be a switch inside the house by the door into the garden. A simple remote control, which you can operate from a fob when you are outside, is certainly worth considering.

BELOW Candles and lanterns create a softer, more romantic atmosphere than electric lighting and are a good way to avoid prohibitive light installation costs.

RIGHT Fire bowls can be powered by gels, gas or solid fuels and provide heat as well as light.

Lighting techniques

- Uplighting trees picks out their trunks and branch networks.

- Backlighting can silhouette plants or a sculpture against a backdrop.

- Spotlighting a key feature makes a dramatic contrast with the surrounding darkness.

- Moonlighting creates a magical silvery effect from a downlighter high up in a tree.

- Washlighting or grazing uses lights at the base of walls to pick out surface texture and cast shadows.

- Downlights are useful for task lighting.

Let there be light

Some fittings are designed to be looked at – think bollards – but often it's the light produced, not the actual fitting, that's the interesting bit. It makes sense to hide some fittings in among plants, or sink them into the ground, but this isn't always possible: the main exceptions are pendant or wall lamps. Candles and lanterns, which always add a touch of magic, are invaluable to supplement electrical fittings. Fire pits fuelled by inflammable gels or even gas should also be considered as a decorative light source rather than as just a heat provider.

SHADOWS AND SILHOUETTES

ABOVE A row of lights at the base of a wall not only picks out the structure itself but throws all the planting in front of it into relief, casting interesting shadows and silhouettes.

COLOURED LIGHTS

LEFT The crisp modern elements of this garden, combined with bold architectural planting, allows for cutting-edge coloured lighting that would possibly look out of place elsewhere.

HANGING LIGHTS

LEFT These white lanterns emit a soft glow that demands attention. They are an installation in their own right but also provide a very practical light source from above.

OUTDOOR LAMPSHADE

BELOW Taking the concept of an outdoor room to extremes, this weatherproof lampshade is suspended from the "ceiling" of the pergola to become the focal point of the seating area.

SPARKLING WATER

ABOVE Moving water has a way of catching light and making it sparkle. Low-voltage lights are anchored in the pool directly below each waterfall.

STEPPING STONES

BELOW Each textured-glass stepping stone is lit from beneath, making it glow and appear to float on the water. Navigation across the pond at night is quite straight-forward as a result.

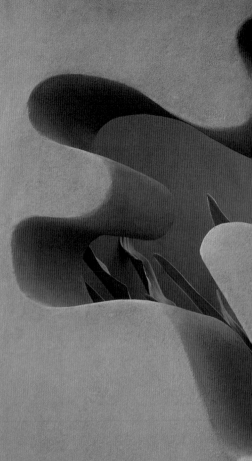

ABOVE Horizontal laths of stone, kept apart by spacers, create defined shadow gaps. These are a powerful contrast to the thick, vertical stems of bamboo, whose dark colour stands out against the pale backdrop.

BELOW Far from acting as a backdrop to something more dramatic, this mosaic provides all the drama itself. The tiny tiles, designed as a piece of artwork, disguise a very ordinary brick wall.

RIGHT The amorphous shape cut into this blue wall becomes an unconventional window, framing the view of the sky and plants beyond, surreptitiously enlisting them as part of the boundary itself.

ABOVE Metal-mesh baskets, known as gabions, could be filled with absolutely anything. Here, they manage to tick a few environmental boxes by using recycled contents and attracting wildlife, which will shelter inside.

Walls and boundaries

Before you start trying to think outside the box, give some thought to the box itself – the boundaries that frame your garden and mark its limits. That fence or wall running around the edge should not be there merely to keep the dog in or unwanted people out. It should be playing a key role in the design make-up of your garden, and the smaller the space, the more pressure there is on it to play a starring role. The boundaries should be every bit as important as a piece of sculpture, a key plant or some designer furniture. And, let's face it, the actual structure of the perimeters can take up very little room yet contribute enormously to the design, so erecting a plain, boring fence is simply an insult to opportunity.

RIGHT The red monolithic wall, backdrop of hardwood timber and slender, stainless steel water chute combine to make up the exciting perimeter of this bijou space, without encroaching upon it in any way.

SOLID WALLS

Material choices for walls are essentially brick, stone or concrete. All should be chosen either to echo or harmonize with the architecture of the building and its surroundings. This often means sourcing materials locally so that they don't jar. Walls are expensive because of the material costs, labour and excavating foundations, but they have a solidity and permanence that can make the investment worthwhile. The cheapest option is concrete blockwork with a cement render, which has a decidedly urban quality. This render may be "self-coloured" using white cement and a particular sand, resulting in a pale, textured patina that is virtually maintenance-free. Otherwise, the render can be painted with masonry paint or a limewash, which is best applied to bare lime-based render, to give a rich patina that changes when it gets wet.

SEASONAL HEDGES

Hedges are living architecture that humanize any concrete jungle where there is too much built structure. They can be bought fully grown, but you are more likely to plant small and then wait for them to grow and thicken. Hedges take up

LEFT Painting walls is an easy and cheap way to improve a garden. The contrasting backdrop emphasizes the shapes and colours of plants.

BELOW Sheets of pebble-filled metal walkway mesh create a wall when used vertically. Blue acrylic transforms the wall into sculpture.

BUILDING A FRAMEWORK

Boundaries are part of the architecture of a garden – they can set the mood of the entire space. They may be theatrical and dramatic or shy and retiring, allowing whatever is in front to take all the glory. Uplighting or downlighting will pick out texture and details, transforming their appearance at night, when plants and sculpture can be silhouetted against them. There is room for innovation here, perhaps the introduction of a variety of materials, from stone and metal to wood and glass. Steel walkway mesh used vertically (*see* right) forms a slender wall filled with rounded pebbles that push through the bars to catch the sunlight. The result is part wall, part work of art.

RIGHT Masonry paint has a uniform finish but limewash lends a rich patina that changes appearance when wet.

a lot of space, need annual maintenance and somewhere to dispose of the clippings. They can deprive neighbouring plants of moisture and nutrients but, in their favour, they are an excellent habitat for wildlife, provide seasonal change and sometimes flowers and berries.

INEXPENSIVE FENCES

The advantage over walls is that fences are cheaper and easier to erect. They may be off-the-shelf panels or bespoke structures and can be made of the same timber as any decking or furniture within the garden, in order to unite a design. The lines and shadow gaps created by horizontal or vertical boards are interesting details that may echo other features of the garden and prevent the expanse of fencing appearing bland and monotonous.

If you are lumbered with a tired, ordinary fence, and funds or circumstance won't allow you to replace it, apply paint or stain in a very dark colour – black, grey or brown. This allows it to "disappear" and the planting or whatever sits in front becomes the focus. Generally, fences require maintenance, especially softwood ones, which need regular treatment with preservative to prevent rot. Hardwood fences last longer.

Colour choices

- Colours go in and out of fashion but, thankfully, paint isn't permanent and colours are easily changed.

- The right colour will make any planting in front of it stand out dramatically. Black may not seem an obvious choice but it is the king of all boundary colours.

- Try to limit yourself to tints and tones of the same hue to avoid chaotic results.

Considered combinations

In a small space, everything must play more than one role, and boundaries are no exception. They can hide an ugly view, support seats, steps or sculpture, disguise the awkward shape of a plot or celebrate its geometry. Their own shapes, colours and materials could easily link through to other garden highlights. At the very least, they will be a backdrop to planting or other features. A wall with a bold architectural outline makes the perfect foil for soft delicate planting, whereas a visually complex boundary may require strong, simple shapes.

RUST
ABOVE Cantilevered steps project from this dry stone wall. Each has a rusted steel water chute, the colour of which is subtly echoed in the stone.

CURVES
RIGHT Curved walls keep the eye focused on the garden and also have the ability to disguise the shape of the plot.

STONE

LEFT The natural patterns on these huge blocks of stone give each its own character. By combining them with smaller walling stone, the boundary becomes one of the most important features.

NATURAL

BELOW Bamboo, willow and other brushwood comes on a roll. Cheap to buy and quick to install, it can hide a multitude of sins but it does weather fast and life expectancy is short.

CONCRETE BLOCKS

ABOVE Unrendered concrete blocks provide a simple backdrop, saved from banality by the vibrant planting in the foreground that gives it vitality.

COLOURED CIRCLES

BELOW An otherwise plain grey wall is transformed with the integration of coloured glass, bestowing a friendly quality on the stark expanse of concrete.

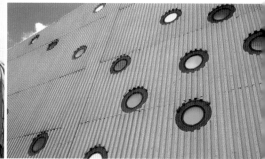

Cohesive colour

Paints and wall finishes can be used to homogenize a space, pulling in a disparate collection of surfaces to unify the design. Alternatively, a single boundary can be picked out with a strong colour to make a feature wall that contrasts with the rest. Hot colours, including reds and oranges, advance forward, drawing the eye immediately, although excessive use can make a space feel smaller. They tend to work better in warmer climates with sunny skies. Conversely, pastel shades and earthy colours recede and can make a space feel larger.

PAINT

ABOVE If you are lumbered with a tired, ordinary fence or shed, and funds or circumstance won't allow you to replace it, the solution is to apply paint or stain to make it part of the overall design.

DARK AND DEEP

LEFT Who knows what the giant marble is for, but the dark-painted wall is a triumph, giving the garden an illusion of depth and picking up the greys in the foliage in front.

RED AND GREEN

RIGHT The architectural outline of a cactus would stand out against any flat background, but against this vibrant red it is particularly striking. Red and green happen to be one of the most contrasting of colour combinations.

DISGUISE

BELOW Modular "green walls" with integral irrigation systems can clad and disguise ugly walls or even buildings, improving the visual environment and providing a home for wildlife.

WOOD

ABOVE Vertical timber boards could be considered rather conventional but they are elevated to the sublime by the addition of circular motifs.

WIRE

BELOW Wire baskets (gabions) are filled with discarded clay tiles and pipes for a contemporary style that cleverly combines cutting-edge cool with rustic charm.

Flooring and surfaces

In theory, you could use virtually any material for surfacing in a garden, as long as it is hard-wearing and weather resistant, so it doesn't deteriorate dramatically with age, and is non-slip to avoid unpleasant accidents. You may also want to walk on it barefoot or in high heels, if you are that way inclined, which would make gravel too uncomfortable and the gaps between decking boards too hazardous. In the end, it will probably come down to some form of timber, stone or concrete, although, if you are adventurous, glass and metal may get a look in.

LEFT A large expanse of paving can be made to feel warmer and more inviting by using small paving units like these brick paviors, which vary in colour and texture.

LEFT Integrating paving and grass prevents excessive wear to the lawn, improves drainage between the stones and creates a very graphic look.

ABOVE Narrow strips of stone have the look of a meandering timber-deck path. Creeping plants conceal the square-cut ends of each stone.

BELOW Smaller units of the same stone material can be inlaid into larger pieces, to make an expanse of ordinary paving far more exciting.

ABOVE The clipped box balls are a good way of bringing greenery into the hard landscaping, with the neat spheres balancing the linear strips of stone and timber.

THE PALETTE

When choosing surfacing materials, consider the material palette of the rest of the garden at the same time. Too many different hard materials can make a small space seem cluttered and restless; too few and it becomes bland and soulless. As a rule of thumb, three is a good average – perhaps stone, timber and painted walls. A fourth material, metal for example, could be introduced as a detail. Be wary of short-lived fashions. Mary Quant once said, "Fashion fades but style remains." A well-designed deck will always look stylish and never go out of date, but the crushed coloured glass of the late 1990s was a mistake that the fashion police should have clamped down on immediately. For a timeless garden that won't date, rely on natural materials. They have been used in gardens for thousands of years and are, undoubtedly, here to stay.

BELOW Timber is very versatile and can be used to make curved pathways. Plants can be grown over the edges of the boards to disguise the cut ends.

LONGING FOR A LAWN?

To some people, a garden isn't a garden if it doesn't have a lawn, and they would probably be happy with a patch of grass no bigger than a double bed. In the end, you have to weigh up whether a lawn is worth the effort to maintain because the weekly mowing, irrigation and repair work can be a real headache. For a lawn to be successful, the drainage underneath must be good and you need a 20cm (8in) depth of decent soil. But small lawns wear out fast, as they have all the traffic concentrated on a limited area. The problem is exacerbated in damp climates, especially if you have dogs and children who come into the house muddy. If the garden is shady, the grass will always struggle, so don't even think about having a lawn.

LEFT Decking must be well designed and use good materials or can look cheap and boring. Square-cut timber "setts" are inlaid into this sophisticated hardwood deck.

BELOW Structural glass panels set against the base of these glass doors enclose strip lighting in the channels beneath.

SPATIAL GYMNASTICS

The surfacing can deceive the eye and make the garden appear distorted. Decking boards or strips of stone running from left to right, for example, can make the space seem wider, but if the boards run up and down, they will take the eye straight to the end and the garden will magically appear lengthened. Similarly, a narrow path will encourage movement along it, while a wide path slows people down.

INSIDE OUT

Blurring the divide between inside and out has become the norm, with level thresholds and large glass doors leading out from the house and directly into the garden.

Materials weather in different ways and at different rates inside and out, and it is almost impossible to get them to match, but it is worth using the same width boards or stones running in the same direction. Ceramic tiles made to look like stone are the only material that doesn't change appearance over time, so they can be used to create a seamless divide.

Character forming

A surface material will impose its character on a garden, although this influence comes not just from the material itself but from the way in which it is used. Hard lines and rigid geometrical shapes dictate a crisp contemporary quality that would be at home in an ultra-modern or minimal garden. And even traditional stone can be diamond-sawn with a honed surface for that cutting-edge look. Curves, organic shapes, intricate patterns and rough hand-cut stone, on the other hand, can nudge things in a more intimate, friendly direction.

LINEAR
ABOVE A strip of low planting and polished black pebbles points finger-like down the garden, introducing a simple sculptural component to a pale limestone terrace.

TREE
LEFT Trees can be grown through decking where they take up very little floor space. Sufficient room must be left around the trunk to allow the tree to grow.

DECKING
RIGHT Different materials can be used to define different areas. Here, the path is decked, while the less-trafficked areas are gravel.

PEBBLE MOSAIC

BELOW Decorating with pebble mosaics dates back thousands of years but they can be used in quite contemporary patterns, the intricate detail working well in a small area.

GREEN GLASS

ABOVE Thin strips of narrow stone have been grouted with green glass chippings, which give a very familiar material a somewhat unusual appearance. Not for everyone, it has to be said.

MESH

BELOW Galvanized walkway mesh introduces interesting detail to an otherwise ordinary deck and can be suspended over water features and planting.

Light versus dark

The hard surfaces in a small garden may take up a high percentage of the total floor area and will either reflect or absorb a huge amount of light. Dark materials, including black granite and slate, can suck the light out of a garden with results that can be stunningly dramatic or rather sombre and claustrophobic – be cautious. Dark stone can also get uncomfortably hot in sunny climates. Conversely, light surfaces make small gardens feel spacious, although the glare from the sun can mean sunglasses are essential.

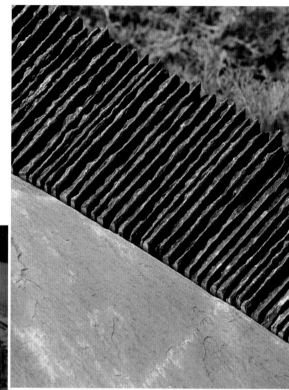

SLATE TILES

ABOVE It pays to use conventional materials in unconventional ways. Slate roof tiles set on edge in concrete use shadows and texture, giving incredible results.

CERAMIC MOSAIC

LEFT A simple mosaic snake motif is made from old ceramic tiles and inlaid into an otherwise plain compacted self-binding gravel floor.

RECLAIMED BRICKS

RIGHT Reclaimed bricks set into gravel hold the loose surface together preventing migration of the stones. Scented plants will spread to fill the gaps and emit a wonderful aroma when bruised lightly underfoot.

STONE SLABS

RIGHT Wide gaps between stone slabs are filled with gravel, allowing spreading plants to soften the hard edges of the steps. The foliage has been carefully selected to harmonize with the stone.

STONE CUBES

ABOVE Limestone setts make beautiful cobbled paving with Mediterranean overtones. The stones can also be used loose as an unconventional mulch on beds.

GRAPHIC

RIGHT Timber boards set into grey gravel create a highly graphic image, emphasized by the fresh green of the adjacent planting.

ABOVE Shade from the sun is provided by a simple canvas canopy, which also offers privacy from above and can be taken down easily in winter.

BELOW This sculptural metal screen becomes the focal point of the garden and gives a sense of enclosure to the seating area.

RIGHT Lightweight fabric mesh has an ethereal quality, echoed in the delicate nature of the planting. Fabric screens should be considered temporary but they are quick and easy to install.

ABOVE Being translucent, glass and perspex let light through, which gives them an added depth.

Screens and canopies

Gardens are our sanctuaries: places for escape, hiding away and relaxation. Most of us will want to do that in private, so we instinctively make an enclosure and shut out the world. We are all animals at the end of the day and we naturally crave shelter and protection. Even if you get on well with the neighbours, you won't want to live on top of each other. Privacy plays a big part in this but protection from the elements is also vital. Whether it is to shade the glare of the sun, escape from the rain or shelter from the wind, there is plenty to be done. Screens and canopies can tick all these boxes and enclose individual rooms within the garden, at the same time making a key contribution to the design.

RIGHT A simple bamboo screen of the right height blocks out an unsightly view at low level, while keeping the view to the sky open and therefore maintaining the feeling of space.

SHIELDING AND SCREENING

Screens can be used to divide the garden up to create the sense of a room, with the screen itself fulfilling the function of a wall. Like our cave-dwelling ancestors, we prefer to sit with our backs to something solid – it makes us feel safe and helps us to relax. But a screen can also be a useful visual backdrop to an area of the garden that we look out on to, giving emphasis to whatever is in the foreground by contrasting with it.

GIMME SHELTER...

A structure that lets light through or over the top will prevent the garden from feeling too enclosed and encourage a feeling of space. Solid screens, including panels of glass or acrylic, will have a wind loading; in other words the wind will put a lot of pressure on them, so they need to be anchored firmly into the ground. They can also create eddy currents and gusts as the wind blows around them, so permeable screens that merely filter or slow the wind down are preferable. Sliding screens and Venetian-type blinds could be installed to give you the best of both worlds.

... AND SANCTUARY

A sense of escapism can be hard to achieve in urban areas or where the density of housing is high. Windows in neighbouring buildings may overlook your garden, or perhaps you can see straight into someone else's bathroom or on to their private terrace. The solution to such situations is rarely to box yourself in, as high walls or fences can feel cage-like. Often the best way to proceed is to create just a sense of privacy: a simple canopy over the terrace will not only shield you from the sun but also hide you from prying eyes. If you get it right, whatever you erect should enhance the overall look of the garden and not appear like an afterthought.

LEFT This simple timber screen made from machined round poles encloses the seating area to create privacy while, at the same time, providing an interesting backdrop.

ABOVE A translucent glass panel allows light through so the small space retains some measure of openness. Plant images turn the screen into an outdoor work of art.

If you are planning a new seating area, go and put a chair in the intended space, sit in it, look about you and identify any potential problems. Are there any overlooking windows? Will you have any shade on sunny days? Is there a prevailing wind howling through a gap between two buildings? Or do you simply feel exposed? An elegant screen could begin to create the sense of a room, with a canopy for the ceiling. Patterned canopies can cast amazing shadows on to the ground beneath, like the dappled shade from certain trees.

RIGHT Vertical timber posts stained dark brown form a partial screen that gently separates two parts of the same garden. The COR-TEN steel background adds drama and colour to the composition.

Cocooned and cool

Your choice of screens and canopies is likely to be influenced by where you live. A temperate climate with wet, windy winters will demand a weather-resistant fabric, ideally a sail material, that can be taken down and stowed away during the winter months – anything that puts the house in shadow should be removed at the end of the year so that the scarce winter sun isn't prevented from entering the living spaces. Dry summer climates mean that even a thin fabric could be sufficient to reduce the harsh effects of the sun.

AWNING
ABOVE A canopy mounted on the house can prevent the sun from glaring into living spaces but it should be easy to take down on gloomy days.

CANVAS
LEFT In hot, dry climates, almost any fabric can make a canopy. The square motifs here cast interesting shadows and echo the rectangular shapes in the hard landscaping.

BAMBOO
RIGHT Bamboo can make an excellent living screen as the side branches can be removed to let light through and expose the elegant canes.

CHAINS
RIGHT Like a giant kinetic sculpture, the weighted chains sway gently in the breeze and shimmer in the sunlight.

ROCK
LEFT A very personal space is created by this arc of metal imprinted with a woodland scene. When you are sitting on the rock, everything behind is totally screened from view.

ACRYLIC SQUARES
BELOW Coloured acrylic squares suspended on wires make an incredibly vibrant screen. They offer privacy, while simultaneously becoming the focus of attention.

RIGHT Recycling at its best: empty wine bottles are drilled through the base and fed by hoses connected to a pump in the reservoir below.

CENTRE RIGHT With an obvious nod to Frank Lloyd Wright's iconic house Fallingwater, the simple stainless-steel trays create an unusual cascade as the water falls from one to the other.

BELOW RIGHT The water in this reflective pool must be kept crystal clear with chemicals and mechanical filtration. Any dirt or debris will spoil the effect.

Water

Water can breathe life into a garden. Water can dance and sing and catch the light from the sky. It can mesmerize and enchant, relax or invigorate. And perhaps because water is one of the four natural elements, people are instantly drawn to it, making it an easy focal point to a garden. Water is also incredibly versatile and can be made to suit almost any design style and readily dictate the mood or atmosphere. It's true that water is often overused, and it doesn't always work, but if you get it right, it can elevate a garden to another level.

ABOVE Water is pumped up through the centre of this slender, curved monolith of black stainless steel and then clings to the sides as it silently flows over the top.

LEFT Natural stone is the ideal backdrop to the water feature. Unlike paintwork, it will improve with age as it gradually accumulates moss and algae.

WATER WORKINGS

Most water features operate on a similar principle: a lower reservoir or pool houses a pump that pushes water through a hose to an upper reservoir, chute or fountain, and the water cascades back down to be recirculated. The pump can also operate a filter, if necessary. These self-contained systems need not be connected to a mains water supply, although it is possible to include an automatic top-up to combat evaporation.

BELOW The higher the waterfall and the more powerful the pump, the louder it all becomes. An inline flow adjuster is useful to limit noise.

where the moving water appears purple. Marginal plants and submerged oxygenating plants will help to keep pond water clean. A balanced ecosystem quickly establishes and a pond will almost look after itself. Floating plants like lilies also shade the water, keeping it cool and reducing algal growth.

SAFETY AND CHILDREN

Children are fascinated by water and it can become the focus of much imaginative play. However, safety is crucial and can be ensured by installing a sturdy metal grid over the water surface to prevent access. This can be disguised by a covering of pebbles, which allow water to percolate down through the grid.

LEFT Like space-age frogspawn or metallic bubbles, these hollow stainless-steel balls float in the water reflecting light and remaining in constant motion thanks to the waterfall.

BELOW This stainless-steel chute has an upper reservoir sitting behind the wall and hidden by planting. A pump recirculates the water.

POOL LINERS

Butyl rubber is one of the best pool liners available, although, on a small scale, it can be difficult to work with, as it's awkward to fold the corners neatly. Far better is fibreglass, or GRP, which is applied *in situ* to a concrete-rendered shell. This can accommodate any shape and makes a reliable waterproof seal around pipes and cables running through the pool wall. Other options are preformed GRP pools or concrete render, which can have specialist sealants applied or be tiled in much the same way as a swimming pool.

KEEPING IT CLEAN

Any water feature requires annual maintenance, to remove leaves and other debris, clean the filters and pumps, and tidy up any planting. A combination of biological filters and ultraviolet clarifiers can keep the water crystal clear, but if you don't have fish, wildlife or plants, swimming pool chemicals are an easy solution. Organic black dyes make the water highly reflective and prevent algal growth but they can't be used with waterfalls or fountains

Water and light

Whether it's a fountain, waterfall or reflective pool, water is great at grabbing our attention. Positioning the feature in natural sunlight is preferable, as it makes the water sparkle, but artificial light is the next best thing. Submersible lights can shine upwards through the water at a descending waterfall, and compact fibre-optics can be placed in a fountain head. Pools of water can be illuminated either from within or by lights shining down on to the surface from above. If the water is moving, dancing ripples can be projected on to walls.

WOOD
ABOVE Timber and water do not mix well as the wood gets watermarked and eventually rots. Here, the stainless-steel chute prevents contact with the water.

STAINLESS STEEL
LEFT Any stainless steel in permanent contact with water should be marine grade or, despite the name, there will still be a risk of rust and staining.

BUCKETS
RIGHT In order to reflect fully in the water's surface, any object positioned on the far side should be as close as possible to the water's edge, and preferably not too tall.

SMALL POOL

BELOW Pools do not need to be huge in order to have any impact. The dark surface of this compact pond stands out dramatically against the bright foliage.

SWIMMING POOL

ABOVE Swimming pools and hot tubs should be thought of as ornamental water features – they can be used to stunning effect in a garden.

CHUTES

BELOW Each individual chute is lit by a submersible light that sits within the base reservoir and shines up through the water as it cascades down.

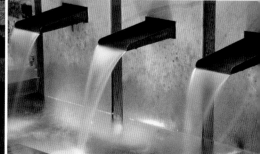

Sight and sound

The scale and power of a water feature has to be considered: an enormous crashing waterfall in a tiny courtyard will destroy any atmosphere, but a feeble bubble of a fountain may have no impact. Fast-moving water will pump out negative ions with the soothing effects of a shower or natural waterfall, whereas silent, gently gliding water will be calming and mesmerizing. A small feature should be brought close to a door or seating area so both sight and sound are easily appreciated; you may even want to be able to reach out and trail your hand in the water.

GLASS

ABOVE Small waterfalls are easily blown by the wind, so should be sheltered – if water escapes from the system, the pump will eventually run dry, unless there is an automatic top-up. The glass chutes allow everything to be seen, so the water must be kept crystal clear.

MOVING WATER

LEFT Mirror-polished stainless steel emphasizes the movement of water, making this curtain waterfall incredibly dramatic.

BUBBLING

LEFT As the water pours from the metal spout, it creates a gentle bubbling sound. The reeds in the pond and an inline filter keep the water clear.

CONCRETE

BELOW This magnificent concrete bowl is part sculpture, part pond. The dwarf lilies shade the surface and prevent the water from overheating in the sun.

METAL SPHERE

ABOVE A skeletal metal sphere echoes the globes of clipped box planted alongside. Water cascades down each rib into a reservoir hidden beneath the pebbles.

BLACK POOL

BELOW The best reflections are achieved with motionless water. Organic dye has made the water inky black and turned its surface into a mirror.

Storage

There is an unwritten law that you will never have enough storage, no matter how big your cupboards. The tiniest garden will need a few tools for maintenance, but even if you have only a broom and some secateurs, they still have to be kept somewhere. And then there's the furniture, cushions and all the other junk we accumulate. Whatever storage you provide, it must be either concealed or turned into an object of beauty. In a large garden, it's easy to hide a shed at the end behind a hedge. In a small space, hiding anything is much more of a challenge.

LEFT Roof terraces are notoriously problematic for storage – everything has to be carried up and down stairs. Here, all available space has been pressed into service.

LEFT Sheds and outdoor cupboards shouldn't be taller than strictly necessary or they will be tricky to conceal. Plants in trays on this roof are perfect camouflage.

ABOVE When space is limited, you need to get creative with your storage solutions, but make sure that everything is as accessible as possible.

BELOW Garden tools can actually be objects of beauty, housed as part storage, part display.

ABOVE Thefts from garden sheds are an increasing problem. A chain running through the handles of everything inside this one makes opportunist theft unlikely.

Boxing clever

Objects that you use every day need to be easily accessible; you shouldn't have to stoop, bend or climb to reach what you are after, or sift through some chaotic jumble. Provide as much space as you can and keep things organized. This applies equally to front gardens as to back yards. Storage for rubbish and recycling is crucial, as it's part of the daily grind, but don't skimp on space. It's infuriating trying to cram rubbish into a bin that's too small, and leaving plastic bags that won't fit lying around is unsightly and a magnet for scavenging animals.

BIKE STORE

ABOVE The overhang of the roof offers some protection from the elements for these bikes, while the vertical storage saves on space. Ingenious integral security locks capture the wheels.

BESPOKE SHED

LEFT A bespoke wooden storage shed not only hides the rubbish bin but also keeps it out of the sun, cutting down on unpleasant smells.

RECYCLING

LEFT This easy-access bin and recycling cupboard even has a green roof to help it blend in with its surroundings.

DECORATIVE

BELOW Garden storage can be decorative. Taking inspiration from a traditional dresser, these combined cupboards and shelves are part storage, part display.

CAMOUFLAGE

ABOVE Conventional shed roofs are at best ugly. Make them attractive with a covering of sedums or other succulents, which grow in virtually no soil and need very little maintenance.

MULTIPURPOSE

BELOW When the lid of this bench seat is down, you wouldn't know that there is essential storage inside.

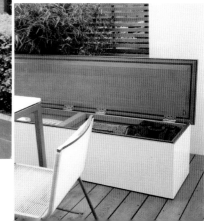

ABOVE Firepits can be quite unattractive when they're not being used, but this curvaceous fire bowl wouldn't spoil the look of any garden, and it can be moved close to wherever you need it.

BELOW You are unlikely to have enough freestanding chairs when you have a party. This seating wall is useful to help deal with the overflow.

RIGHT Rainproof, even stainproof and sheltered from the sun, this stainless-steel structure is quite literally an outdoor kitchen for those who are really serious about entertaining.

ABOVE Work surfaces need to be wide enough and, ideally, at about 90cm (35in) high, just as they would be in your kitchen. Storage underneath is useful, and you might even decide to include an outdoor fridge and a sink.

Cooking, eating and heating

Eating outside is one of life's pleasures and everything should be designed to make it easy, otherwise the pleasure can quickly turn to pain. Cooking and dining areas need to be close to the kitchen so that taking all the required paraphernalia outside doesn't become a chore. Seating, tables and as much of the equipment as possible should be either close at hand or permanent features. If the whole exercise requires superhuman effort, you'll seldom do it. Cool evenings are much more enjoyable with some warmth, but gas-powered heaters are an eco non-starter and also very unattractive. There are other more romantic ways to keep warm, which will actually improve the look of your garden.

RIGHT Psychologists agree that sitting round a fire is incredibly relaxing. Harking back to our cave-dwelling days, it fulfils some basic primeval human need.

Comfort food

When space is at a premium, there's no point trying to shoehorn in a huge table and masses of furniture. Having less space on an outdoor table than you might expect inside is perfectly acceptable. It's far more important to give room to the seating. Chairs shouldn't be precariously balanced on the edge of a terrace or pond, or have to be pushed backwards and forwards to allow people to leave the table. The furniture you choose shouldn't be too bulky because it will crowd a small garden and be difficult to move around.

ELEGANCE
ABOVE There's no reason why cooking, dining and storage can't be combined in a stylish, elegant way that doesn't detract from the overall look of the garden.

SLATTED ROOF
LEFT Cooking a meal outside can mean standing in the sun for considerable lengths of time, so shade should always be provided.

STONE SURFACES
RIGHT Stone table tops and work surfaces have to be treated with sealant, as wine, olive oil and lemon juice can leave unsightly stains.

LARGE GATHERINGS

BELOW This bench seating will accommodate a multitude of people gathered around the fire, which can also be used for cooking.

HANGING UTENSILS

ABOVE This really is an outdoor kitchen for the serious chef. The stainless-steel frame ensures every implement and utensil is to hand and that herbs are within arm's reach.

FACE TO FACE

BELOW Cooking and preparing food can be a sociable affair but only if the cook is facing his or her guests. Conversation is made easier with the seating arranged nearby.

RIGHT Red-tinged grasses wave in the breeze like a flickering candle flame atop slender, powder-coated, grey containers.

CENTRE RIGHT Tall pots need squat plants, otherwise the centre of gravity will be too high, causing them to overbalance.

BELOW RIGHT Cacti and succulents require relatively shallow soil. Free drainage is their main requirement.

Pots and containers

Pots? Containers? These are both words that merely suggest a utilitarian receptacle in which to grow a plant, yet the receptacle itself is often a thing of great beauty and every bit as important as any plant. The right containers (let's stick with that word for now) can be key features of a garden and, in some cases, provide part of the structure – this can be true even if they remain unplanted. What this all means is that they shouldn't just be an afterthought or an accessory used to dress the stage but instead should become an integral part of the set.

ABOVE The brushed, stainless-steel troughs are bolted to the wall edge and form the parapet, dispensing with the need for any form of railing.

LEFT The spiky yucca echoes the angular shapes of the rusty steel, wall-mounted container, which harmonizes with the orange wall.

MATERIAL CONSIDERATIONS

Metal is incredibly versatile, as it can be fabricated and painted to suit the requirements of the site and scheme exactly.

Plastic pots are lightweight and therefore easily shifted around, making them ideal for balconies and rooftops. Fibreglass and resin pots are on the whole superior, though, and modern techniques allow for some good-looking, high-quality products.

Terracotta is porous, which means that plants rarely become waterlogged but they also dry out fast. This material tends to be most suited to traditional schemes. Ceramic pots are quite versatile and easy to clean but, like terracotta, can be damaged by frost.

Reconstituted stone, terrazzo and concrete are all very heavy but age well.

SOIL AND DRAINAGE

Drainage holes in the base of any container are essential to prevent waterlogging, and a layer of stone chippings will improve drainage further.

LEFT Being porous, terracotta pots are ideal for succulents and other plants that don't like being wet at the roots as excess water can evaporate through the sides.

BELOW Pots don't necessarily have to be receptacles for plants. A row of empty urns set against the right backdrop is every bit as interesting as a row of planted pots.

PLANT FLEXIBILITY

Plants in pots can be rotated to bring in seasonal colour and scent, or wheeled out of the way when the plant stops flowering and has a bit of annual downtime. This is easier with small containers, although larger ones can be fitted with castors or sat on wheeled trays. Heavy immovable pots are best planted with evergreen plants that will perform all year. Containers also give you the luxury of bringing highlights or colour to areas where there is no actual soil, perhaps on a roof, in a basement or on a large paved terrace. They let you control the soil so you can grow plants that would normally find a part of the garden too dry or perhaps of the wrong acidity. Difficult shady corners can play host on a temporary basis to flowering plants that usually need plenty of sun.

RIGHT Metal containers can overheat in summer and freeze plant roots in winter. Use polystyrene sheets to provide insulation.

Peat-based composts are ideal for seasonal planting, although loam-based compost is generally better for shrubs and trees – as they are heavier, the pots are less likely to blow over in wind. Ideally, trees should have a 90–120cm (3–4ft) depth of soil, ordinary shrubs 60–90cm (2–3ft), annuals 30cm (12in) and small alpines and succulents as little as 10cm (4in).

WATERING AND FEEDING

A plant in a container will be hungrier and thirstier than one with its feet in the ground. Automatic irrigation drippers on micropipes threaded up through drainage holes can save a lot of hassle with hoses and cans. However, you could choose plants that can stomach a little hardship, such as succulents. There are also many plants with thick glossy leaves that don't lose much water through the leaf surfaces. A container in full sun or in the wind will dry out much more quickly than one in a sheltered shady spot. A mulch on the soil surface will cut down evaporation – this could be pebbles or ornamental stone chippings. A slow-release granular fertilizer should be mixed into the compost when the container is newly planted or forked into the compost surface in spring.

Pot priorities

- Choose pots primarily for their sculptural or architectural qualities rather than their plant-holding abilities. Some pots actually have more impact without plants.

- Have a strong vision – a row of three or four statuesque containers is far superior to an eclectic assortment of old pots from a previous garden.

- Use a pot rather than plants to inject colour into a space.

Scene-setters

The most successful design schemes are linked either with the plants, their containers or both, thereby creating the greatest impact and drama. The background is crucial to achieving this. A plain, simple backdrop will show plants and pots in the foreground to best advantage. It is even worth considering repainting a wall to complement the containers in front for the sake of unity and cohesion. Above all, pots and plants must suit the character of your garden space to avoid looking like an afterthought.

ARCHITECTURAL
ABOVE The succulent agave is a piece of living sculpture that demands an equally architectural container. This cast-iron pot links with the COR-TEN steel wall behind.

CONTRAST
RIGHT These slender orange pots, striking against a lavender wall, are lightweight enough to be brought indoors in the winter in a cold climate, to protect the tender echeveria.

DIFFERENCES
LEFT Even though these containers are different colours and contain different kinds of plant, their identical shapes ensure harmony.

LINE-UP
BELOW Clipped box balls and terracotta pots are as traditional as they come, although the repetition gives the balcony a contemporary twist.

BLACK BACKDROP
ABOVE The black wall is the perfect backdrop, throwing the pots and cream-striped yuccas into sharp relief.

SCULPTURAL POTS
BELOW Containers can be incredibly sculptural in their own right and don't necessarily need to be planted up.

ABOVE These solid, curvaceous chairs were chosen not only for their comfort but also for their bold shape, which stands out among the soft colour-themed planting.

BELOW This sophisticated bench, which picks up on the horizontal lines of the boundary fence and suits the geometry of the entire garden, is both functional and aesthetic.

RIGHT Low-slung furniture is ideal for relaxing or drinking a cup of coffee but not so practical for dining, when more upright chairs and a higher table are needed.

ABOVE Is this a bench that's a sculpture or a sculpture you can sit on? In a small space, multifunctionality is vital.

Outdoor furniture

You probably remember those dreadful, cheap, white plastic patio chairs that not so long ago were in virtually every garden in the world. Well, thankfully, that dreadfulness has been consigned to the dustbin of garden history and, with revolutions in design and technology, there is now a colossal amount of well-designed furniture for outdoor use. Some of it is mass-produced and affordable, but there also are expensive "designer" pieces and even hand-crafted individual works designed for a particular space. There really is something available for every taste and every budget. However, making that choice requires careful thought and consideration for how your new furniture will work within the garden.

RIGHT Solid lumps of green oak quickly turn silver as they dry out, splitting and twisting to give extra character to the seat.

WHERE TO START

In an ideal world, you would have furniture to suit every purpose: a dining table and chairs, something comfortable for reading, like an outdoor armchair or sofa, and then, perhaps, a couple of loungers for lying in the sun. But, in reality, even a large garden would struggle to accommodate this much furniture without looking like a showroom, so in a small garden you have to make some big decisions about where your priorities lie.

MAKING COMPROMISES

A stool or a bench with a hard seat may be okay if you're just going to sit down for a quick cup of coffee or even a bite to eat. But if you want to linger, you will need a chair with a back and probably some sort of cushion. The most flexible solution is to have a normal-height table and stackable, comfortable, dining-style chairs, which keep you upright enough to eat but allow you to sit back and relax properly. This furniture should not be too big or cumbersome – the more slender it is, the better, so that it will integrate with the garden rather than dominate it. Alternatively, you may prefer to go for the comfortable option – big, cushioned, sofa-type chairs and a low table, but this essentially rules out proper meals and means that you will end up eating off your lap.

MATERIAL QUESTIONS

You also need to consider the maintenance of your furniture, how it will survive the weather and what it feels like to touch. The climate where you live will influence your choice – metal, for example, can get very hot and also very cold.

Wood is the classic material for outdoor furniture, always a comfortable temperature to sit on and it works with most styles of garden. Sunlight will eventually turn all wood silver and there is no product to prevent this unless you routinely sand and stain and varnish. Essentially, if you don't like the silvering, wood is not for you.

LEFT A contemporary classic furniture piece – part chair, part sculpture – is integral to the overall design of this garden.

Moulded-plastic tables and chairs are now frequently well designed, cheap, robust, comfortable and even colourful. However, the biggest recent innovation has been plastic "rattan", a woven material that looks very natural and stands up to any weather. Ordinary, untreated fabrics are a problem in all but the driest climates yet they are the best way to inject a little comfort and colour into the furniture and, therefore, the garden. Shower-proof Teflon-coated fabrics are available but you should still store them away during the wetter months.

BELOW Loungers can be bulky and may need to be moved frequently as you chase the sun or the shade around a garden, so wheels are a must-have.

RIGHT This simple wire-framed furniture takes up very little room and won't dominate the garden. The lightweight stools are easily moved around.

Keep it simple

- Freestanding furniture should be easy to move, and chairs, ideally, stackable for convenient storage.

- Ceramic or glass table tops are easily cleaned, whereas timber and certain stones can mark easily. Cushion covers should be removable and washable.

- Furniture that can be left outside in all weathers, so you can sit out whenever the mood takes you, makes life a whole lot easier.

- When choosing furniture, remember that it is a key feature of the garden design, not merely something to sit on.

- Some types of furniture, particularly loungers, take up a huge amount of floor space. Check that the furniture fits before you buy.

Works of art

Some of the most expensive outdoor furniture looks absolutely fantastic yet it is often a triumph of form over function and quite uncomfortable, so you should always try before you buy. Commissioning a bespoke design results in a unique piece of furniture that not only embodies all the qualities of an artwork or sculptural installation but also reflects your personality and fits your garden space perfectly. In truth, this is not necessarily cost-efficient but a really well-designed piece takes the whole thing on to another level.

FOLDING CHAIR

ABOVE Space-saving at its best: this adjustable chair folds down and disappears into the decking, brilliantly resolving any storage problems.

GLASS LOUNGER

LEFT Structural glass is incredibly strong and versatile. Here, the bluish-green tinge sits well among the silvery foliage.

ROOF RECLINERS

RIGHT This ingenious roof garden twists the bands of decking into waves at one end and curls them up at the other, to make permanent recliners.

NEW-AGE PLASTIC

RIGHT Modern, mass-produced plastic furniture is far better-looking than it once was and can be a relatively inexpensive way to give your garden a contemporary edge.

SCULPTURAL CHAIRS

LEFT At first glance, the throne-like, high-backed chairs appear to be a sculptural installation, with seating an almost incidental function.

INTEGRATED LOUNGERS

BELOW Loungers eat up the space – they're at least 2m (6½ft) long – so here they have been cleverly integrated into the planting instead of cluttering the terrace.

INDEX

PICTURE CREDITS

Mitchell Beazley would like to acknowledge and thank the following for providing images for publication in this book.

Key: a above, b below, c centre, d design by, l left, r right

2 Interior Archive/Helen Fickling/d Catherine Heatherington; 7 Helen Fickling/d Catherine Heatherington; 8 Harpur Garden Images/Jerry Harpur/d Tim and Dagny DuVal; 10 Andrew Lawson/d Hadrian Whittle; 12 al Harpur Garden Images/d Christopher Bradley-Hole, ar Harpur Garden Images/Jerry Harpur/d Luciano Giubbilei, bl Estrada from Gloster Furniture Ltd, br Marianne Majerus/d Christopher Bradley-Hole; 13 Helen Fickling/d Andy Sturgeon; 14 a Andrew Lawson Photography/Torie Chugg/d Kate Gould; b Garden World Images/Modeste Herwig/d CBH; 15 Photolibrary Group/Garden Picture Library/Ron Sutherland/d Jack Merlo; 16 Andrew Lawson Photography/Torie Chugg/d Linda Upson and Carole Syms; 17 a Helen Fickling/d Catherine Heatherington, b Helen Fickling/d Wayne and Geraldine Hemingway; 18 b, 19 al Interior Archive/Helen Fickling/d Andy Sturgeon; 19 ar, bl and br Helen Fickling/d Andy Sturgeon; 20 l Andrew Lawson/d Thomas Hoblyn, ar Jerry Pavia, br David Sarton/Octopus Publishing Group/d Boardman Gelly and Co; 21 a Photolibrary Group/George Gutenberg/InsideOutPix, b Marianne Majerus/d Jilayne Rickards; 22 Derek St Romaine/d Rachel Ewer; 23 a Helen Fickling/d Wayne and Geraldine Hemingway, b Interior Archive/Helen Fickling/d Dean Herald/Fleming's Nurseries; 24 Alamy/Elizabeth Whiting and Associates; 25 a Harpur Garden Images/Jerry Harpur/d Raymond Jungles, b Garden Collection/Liz Eddison/d Claire Whitehouse; 26–27 Marianne Majerus/d Alastair Howe Architects; 28 al Jerry Pavia, ar Helen Fickling/Flora International, Montreal, bl Science Photo Library/Mike Comb/d Matt Noakes and Matt Jarvis, br Garden Collection/Liz Eddison/d Boardman and Gelly; 29 Andrew Lawson; 30 Helen Fickling/d Jack Merlo/Float Garden, Fleming's Nurseries; 31 a Harpur Garden Images/Jerry Harpur/d Chrisptoph Swinnen, b Interior Archive/Fritz von der Schulenburg/d Geordie Ferguson; 32 Clive Nichols/d Erick de Maeijer and Jane Hudson; 33 Garden Collection/Liz Eddison/d Lucy Hunter; 34 l Andrew Lawson Photography/Torie Chugg /d Jill Brindle, r Garden Collection/Liz Eddison/d Stuart Perry; 35 Andrew Lawson/d Christopher Bradley-Hole; 36–37 courtesy Andrea Cochran Landscape Architecture/d Andrea Cochran; 38 al Garden Collection/Liz Eddison/d Stephen Hall, ar Harpur Garden Images/Jerry Harpur/d Sam Martin, bl Harpur Garden Images/Jerry Harpur/d Thomas Hoblyn, br Garden Collection/Jonathan Buckley/d Lizzie Taylor and Dawn Isaac; 39 Harpur Garden Images/d Corinne Layton; 40–41 Helen Fickling/Merrill Lynch, RHS Chelsea/d Andy Sturgeon; 42 a Andrew Lawson/d Casper Gabb, bl Interior Archive/Mark Luscombe-Whyte/d Jean-Francois Bodin, br Derek St Romaine/d Cleve West; 43 a and b Andrew Lawson/d James Aldridge; 44 Harpur Garden Images/d Corinne Layton; 45 a Red Cover/Practical Pictures, b courtesy Paul Cha Architect/photo Da Lou Zha/d Cha and Innerhofer; 46–47 Harpur Garden Images/Jerry Harpur/d Philip Nixon; 48–49 Clive Nichols/d Stephen Woodhams; 50 al Alamy/Steven Wooster/d Michelle Osbourne, ar Garden Exposures/Andrea Jones/d Joe Swift and Samantha Woodroofe, bl Marianne Majerus/d Declan Buckley, br Photolibrary Group/Garden Picture Library/Steven Wooster/d A Paul; 51 Arcaid/Morley von Sternberg/d USE Architects/Jo Hagan; 52 a Red Cover/Michael Freeman/d Tsuyoshi Nagasaki, b Red Cover/Tim Evan-Cook; 53 Marianne Majerus/d Paul Cooper; 54 l Harpur Garden Images/Jerry Harpur/d Ulf Nordfjell, r Gap Photos/Jerry Harpur/d Brian Berry for Dan Pearson; 55 Harpur Garden Images/Jerry Harpur/d Stephen Crisp; 56 a courtesy Andy Sturgeon/photo Andrew Or/d Andy Sturgeon, b, 57 all Harpur Garden Images/Jerry Harpur/d Andy Sturgeon; 58 a Red Cover/Practical Pictures, bl Andrew Lawson/d James Aldridge, br Gap Photos/Jerry Harpur/d Vladimir Sitta; 59 a Alamy/John Glover/d Nathalie Charles, b Andrew Lawson/d James Aldridge; 60 Harpur Garden Images/d Bernard Hickie; 61 a courtesy Andy Sturgeon/d Andy Sturgeon; b Harpur Garden Images/Jerry Harpur/d Jeff Dutt and Philippa O'Brien; 62 Gap Photos/Jerry Harpur/d Philip Nash; 63 a Gap Photos/Jerry Harpur/d Andrea Cochran, b Gap Photos/Jerry Harpur/d Stephen Woodhams; 64 a and b, 65 all courtesy Andy Sturgeon/d Andy Sturgeon; 66 al Helen Fickling/d Paula Ryan, ar Derek St Romaine/d Philip Nash, bl Garden Exposures/Andrea Jones/d Joe Swift, br Garden Exposures/Andrea Jones/d Matt Vincent and Wayne Page; 67 Photolibrary Group/Garden Picture Library/Susan Seubert; 68 Garden World Images/Jacqui Dracup/d Scenic Blue Design Team; 69 a Photolibrary Group/Garden Picture Library/Gil Hanly, b Andrew Lawson/d Wynniatt-Husey Clarke; 70 Garden Exposures/Andrea Jones/d Samantha Woodroofe and Joe Swift; 71 a Andrew Lawson/d Cyrus Design, b Garden Collection/Liz Eddison/d Harpuk Design; 72 a, 73 al Interior Archive/Helen Fickling; 72 b, 73 ar, bl and br Helen Fickling/d Andy Sturgeon; 74 al Red Cover/Jason Lowe/d Michael Reeves, ar Red Cover/Michael Freeman/d Masayuki Yoshida, bl Harpur Garden Images/d Martin Sacks, br Marianne Majerus/d Dominique Lubar; 75 Photolibrary Group/Photononstop/Guy Bouchet-Cardinale; 76 a Garden Collection/Jonathan Buckley/d Diarmuid Gavin, b Marianne Majerus/d Claire Mee Designs; 77 Nicola Browne/d Ross Palmer; 78 Michael Freeman/d Yoshiji Takehara; 79 l Arcaid/Nicholas Kere/d Belsize Architects, r Garden Collection/Jonathan Buckley/d Marianne McKiggan; 80 a Garden Collection/Marie O'Hara/d Kate Gould, b Photolibrary Group/Claire Takacs/d Kate Gould; 81 al and br Garden Collection/Liz Eddison/d Kate Gould, ar Gap Photos/Mark Bolton/d Kate Gould, bl Alamy/Mark Bolton/d Kate Gould; 82 a Arcaid/Alan Weintraub/d Marcio Kogan, bl Derek St Romaine/d Cleve West, sculpture by Johnny Woodford, br Gap Photos/Leigh Clapp/Chainhurst Cottages; 83 a Gap Photos/Brian North/d Alistair Kirt Bayford, b Elizabeth Whiting and Associates/Rodney Hyett; 84 courtesy Andrea Cochran Landscape Architecture/photo Marion Brenner/d Andrea Cochran; 85 a Red Cover/Michael Freeman, b Clive Nichols/d Michel Semini; 86 l Harpur Garden Images/Jerry Harpur/d Jenny Jones, r Gap Photos/Leigh Clapp/Buchanan Garden; 87 View Pictures/Philip Bier; 88 b, 89 a Harpur Garden Library/Jerry Harpur/d Terragram; 88 a, 89 bl and br Terragram/Walter Glover/d Terragram; 89 al Terragram/Vladimir Sitta/d Terragram; 90–91 Helen Fickling/d Raymond Jungles Inc, mosaic mural by Debra Yates; 92 al Helen Fickling/d Andy Sturgeon, ar Garden Collection/Nicola Stocken Tomkins/d Andy Sturgeon, bl Marianne Majerus/d Christopher Bradley-Hole, br Garden World Images /Modeste Herwig; 93 Garden World Images/Anne Green-Armytage/d Jennifer Hirsch; 94 a Gap Photos/Howard Rice, b Gap Photos/Marcus Harpur; 95 Gap Photos/Jonathan Buckley/d Pam